EVELYN FOSTER

MURDER OR FRAUD

ON THE NORTHUMBERLAND MOORS.

ROBERT DIXON

WOLF'S NICK PUBLISHING

Copyright © 2011 Robert Dixon
All rights reserved.

Dedicated to the people of Otterburn
Past and present
Who have lived with the mystery.

CONTENTS.

Acknowledgements.

Introduction.

Chapter 1   Foundations And Roots.

Chapter 2   The Story.

Chapter 3   A Police Presence.

Chapter 4   The Journey To Nowhere.

Chapter 5   The Invisible Man And The Mystery Woman.

Chapter 6   The Inquest: A Battle Of Wills.

Chapter 7   Conclusions: Unravelling The Tangled Web.

Select Bibliography.

Photographic Credits.

ACKNOWLEDGEMENTS.

As always with a book project such as this a large amount of help was received from an equally large amount of people. Without their help a book such as this could not have been written in the first place. Many of their names will not appear here but my thanks go to them anyway. A number of people from Otterburn and its district put forward ideas, recollections and other bits but requested that their names were not to be revealed: Their help and requests are acknowledged with thanks to all however small your help was.

There are also a number of establishments who grave great assistance and, first and foremost among these are the Northumberland Archive at Woodhorn, holders of the official files on Evelyn Foster. The staff must have been worn out carrying the files back and forth over two years or so as well as answering questions that may have appeared odd at times.

Among others who provided much help were: Joe Walton of Troughend farm, Jean McLean of Paisley Library, Kate Cullen and Clare Broomfield of English Heritage: Ruth Smith of Hexham Library who provided help way above the call of duty. Thanks are also due to Jane Walton and Rev Marion Penfold of Otterburn. Also to the many people of Otterburn who gave another 'strange man' as I wandered around their village. To others I know I have missed out, thank you all, it was a great, thought provoking journey as well as a learning curve.

I dream of moor, and misty hill,

Where evening closes dark and chill...

What have those lonely mountains worth revealing.

Emily Brontë.

INTRODUCTION.

The County of Northumberland is the fifth largest county in England: most of it however, tends to be of a rural nature. Due to the proximity of the Scottish border the history of Northumberland was steeped in violence for most of the time. The area around Redesdale that sits on the edge of Northumberland's National Park is situated in the very heart of Border Country. The area known for its outstanding beauty masks its own brand of historical lawlessness and violence. However, by 1931 peace had settled on Redesdale and the town of Otterburn, a village that had given its name to the battle fought there in 1388. The whole area had become a quiet backwater, a place in which to spend a quiet holiday in the suspended animation that followed The First World War, the war to end all wars.

On 6 January 1931, Twelfth Night; an incident was to occur that literally forced this peaceful backwater village out of its cosy slumber onto the pages, not only of the British press but also the World's press. A young woman had been brutally done to death in a suspected case of murder by fire on the wild moorland near her home in rural Northumberland. The background was set with the wild moorland and its backdrop of the bleak, Ottercops Hills; only a couple of miles away stood a gibbet on the Steng Cross, a relic of justice in the aftermath of a murder in days gone by. The incident had taken place at Wolf's Nick on a typical Redesdale, winter's night: everything was in place for a newspaper feast.

In the aftermath of the case it was the police who bore the brunt of the outcome due, it was said, mainly to their incompetence. However, as with everything else, it is easy to make someone a scapegoat in order to gloss over what really happened and so perpetuate the myth. One or two attempts have been made to cast a light on the case. One of these was the book by Jonathan Goodman: 'The Burning Of Evelyn Foster' 1977 which presents the story in a reasonable, balanced way. The affects of the press over the years have only served to muddy the waters as they have only used their own sources which they passed on as fact; something it certainly was not, even at the time. The television has also made an attempt with; 'In Suspicious Circumstances: The Man Who Melted Away' in 1994. However, the only thing this had in common with the Foster case was the names of the characters. It was, in effect, what is known as 'faction'. Faction only plays to an audience who take it as fact, as such; legends and myths are born and perpetuated making it ever harder to dispel them.

So, what really happened on the Twelfth Night of 1931? I have been fortunate enough to have used the official documents of the Foster case now in the Northumberland Archives. I was also to note that these documents had been locked away under the seventy-five years closure rule; no one else had used them in that time. The following is not a criminal investigation but looks at the events of 6 January 1931, from a historical perspective; that is what the Foster case is now, a piece of Northumbrian history. I have also made use of various sources and tools available from the genealogy perspective. This has given many of the central figures as well as buildings and the area involved, a more rounded, in depth view. The result, I feel sure, gives the whole Foster case a much more in depth and creditable view.

CHAPTER ONE.

FOUNDATIONS AND ROOTS.

The road from Newcastle to Otterburn is a normal, rural, countryside road until it reaches the village of Knowesgate; the actual village stands a bit back from the main road. From here the road climbs and turns slightly left, on right and left, the land is agricultural though sparse. About one and a half miles further on the road cuts through a gap in an outcrop of rock; to the traveller, it's as if the outcrop of rock acted as a wall with a gate, once through the cut in the rock the land opens up to a very different vista. The traveller is now faced with wide open, wild moorland, some of the wildest to be seen in the English Borders as the green gives way to the brown and black of the heather covered moorland. The moors are full of bogs and marsh-land that are crisscrossed by small gullies and streams. In the distance lies Harwood Forrest and visible to the North West is the Steng Cross with its gibbet acting as a grim reminder to a previous murder in this area. The bleak and barren land in between is known as *Ottercops Moss*. The cut through the rocky outcrop is known locally, as it does not appear on any map, as Wolf's Nick. The name probably derives from the nearby Wolf Crag. It is this bleak area, some one-hundred and twenty yards to the north of Wolfs Nick that was the scene of a crime on 6 January 1931.

Looking to the north-west, the road stretches to Otterburn, some six miles distant. Although this is one of the main routes to Scotland the dimensions of the road do not indicate this as it twists and turns snake-like in its plunge down into Redesdale, at times forcing the traffic down to a mere thirty miles per hour in order to negotiate some of the many severe turns. This area has hardly changed at all since 1931 and the only real difference is the increased volume of traffic. Open and wild the land may be but the traffic is incessant. In 1931, this was one of the main through roads to Scotland. However, motor transport was not so common and the traffic on this road would be very light in comparison to that of today. Major road or not, this road would have been a very lonely one on a winter's night in 1931.

The surrounding landscape around Wolf's Nick is little changed since 1931. The verge here has very little height, however, once crossed it has a drop of around five feet before it hits a fence; contemporary photographs appear to show that there was no fence in 1931 which is not surprising as many roads in the area were unfenced even as late as the 1970s. A hundred and twenty yards or so to the north of Wolf's Nick lies the patch of moorland where the deed, whatever it was, was carried out in 1931. When photographs of 1931 are compared with those of today, there is little, if any change in the landscape. The black and white photographs of 1931 appearing to make the landscape even more bleak. A small right of way passes close to the scene and although this area is well out in the 'sticks', on my first visit in 2007 the only sign of modernity visible, apart from the passing traffic, was the usual discarded cans and bottles and, surprisingly ironic, the remains of a burnt out car. The ground is boggy and a stream cuts across at an angle from left to right; it was here that Evelyn Foster's car finally came to rest. This was the scene of the landscape flashed to all parts of the country, courtesy of the press of the day, as the murder scene along with its headline grabbing title, Wolf's Nick, grabbed the front pages.

Otterburn was, and still is, only a small village and has little changed over the years from 1931. The village main street borders the main Jedburgh to Newcastle road that dissects the little village. A time-traveller from 1931 would have little difficulty recognising the village today. Buildings that were to play a central part in the events of 1931 still survive today. Otterburn Tower, a private residence of Mrs Howard Pease, widow of the local antiquarian, the late Howard Pease, still stands sentinel above the banks of the Otter Burn. For a few weeks in 1931, it was to take on the role of headquarters or incident room, for Northumberland County Constabulary as it began its search for the murderer of Evelyn Foster.

Otterburn Bridge crosses the Otter Burn, a burn that dissects the village as well as giving the village its name, the bridge recognisable as such merely by a small bump in the road and its two balustrade sides. The two balustrade sides, at first glance, could be easily mistaken for walls. It was at this point, if we believe Evelyn's deathbed statement, that she had her second fateful meeting with the 'strange man'. It was also the place where another two witnesses, both women, had encountered a 'strange man' on the tree-shaded Otterburn Bridge. Were these three men one and the same at different times or were they three separate people perhaps blissfully unaware that they had been singled out as suspects in a murder case? It is important to note that, from that bridge an observer can see as far as just beyond the church. On a night such as the Twelfth Night of 1931, the lights from Evelyn's car, as it stood outside the 'Kennels', would have easily been observed by anyone standing in the vicinity of the bridge. Likewise, a man standing there would have easily been picked out by a car driving down the street from the 'Kennels'. There was no street lighting in Otterburn at this time.

The 'Percy Arms', much modernised and enlarged still stands hard by the Otter Burn. Taking its name from Harry Hotspur Percy of the Battle of Otterburn fame. The Percy Arms is now a restaurant and hotel. In times past, the 'Percy Arms' was once a coaching Inn and it was here that the coach, the 'Chevy Chase' stopped on its way from Newcastle to Jedburgh and again on its return later in the day. The 'Percy Arms' has had long associations with travellers as they passed north or south. In 1931 it still served coaching travellers as a stopping off point for the Foster busses as well as a place often frequented by Evelyn Foster for the passing on of any messages in connection with her taxi business. The 'Percy Arms' was to play a pivotal role in the events of the Twelfth Night, 1931 for it was here that the 'strange man', after apparently walking down the main street of Otterburn, was to visit in further pursuit of a lift to Newcastle.

Standing alongside the 'Percy Arms' is the 'War Memorial Hall'; almost everyone in Britain was familiar, in 1931, with this hall and, the drama played out within it. Apart from its obvious use within the village, the 'War Memorial Hall' doubled as a village hall or, in modern day language, a community hall. In this capacity it was used for various parties, meetings and dances and, was of particular use around the Christmas period for the various festivities.

WAR MEMORIAL HALL

However, the knowledge covering the activities in January 1931 had spread worldwide: the following from "*The Sydney Morning Herald*", Friday, 9 January, 1931: '*Fiendish Murder; Girl Burnt To Death'*. Evelyn Foster, a pretty brunette, aged 28, daughter of a garage proprietor, was found dying beside her blazing motor-car on a lonely moor near Otterburn, a few miles from the Scottish border, last night. Before dying in her father's arms, she described in whispers how she had been murdered. "On the way home", she said, "a stranger requested a lift, saying that he had come from Scotland. I took him as far as Belsay, when he asked me to turn back, which I did. At Kirkwhelpington he stunned me with a blow to the head, and threw me back into the car, which he set on fire and pushed over a steep bank. I remember being jolted across the moor, and crawling from the blazing car". A bus driver saw the blaze and found Miss Foster terribly injured, with her clothes burned off.'

A similar article, carrying a report on the inquiry was to appear in New Zealand's "*Evening Post*" issue of 5 February, 1931, under the headline: "*Murder of Girl; Verdict at Inquest*". At the inquest of Evelyn Foster the jury returned a verdict of murder against an unknown person. It is believed that the person poured petrol on Miss Foster and set fire to her. Evelyn Foster, daughter of a garage proprietor, was found dying on 6th January beside her blazing motor-car on a lonely moor near Otterburn on the Scottish border. Before decease she told her father that she had been assaulted and murdered by a man she had given a lift to. He threw her in the back of the car, set fire to it, and pushed it over the bank.' Many other newspapers in Australia and New Zealand were to carry reports of January 1931 and even more so, of the drama acted out in the ‚War Memorial Hall' in Otterburn.

Across the road from the 'War Memorial Hall' stands the bothy, a building set back from the road; one of five houses in a terrace. As Joseph Foster's business began to expand, he needed a larger workforce. Most of the people of Otterburn worked within the farming industry or the few shops and larger houses gardens: the other main employer in Otterburn was Otterburn Mill. As a result, Joseph Foster had to import his workforce mainly from various parts of the County but also from other parts of the Country as well as Scotland. Dwelling accommodation for these men had to be found so; he bought a house and converted it into what became the bothy; a simple place basically for his workforce to sleep. One of the men who lived in the bothy was George Philipson, a joiner by trade, who looked after all the woodwork on the Foster busses. George Philipson was a friend of Evelyn Foster, some say her fiancé in all but name, true or not, he was at least trusted by the Foster family. The bothy, being inhabited by males, mainly unmarried, gained a bit of a reputation of being somewhat rough; this may or may not have had a bearing on the events of 6 January, 1931.

A little further along the street, on the north side, stands the church dedicated to *St John*. Today, probably because of its country situation, it is one of the few churches that are left open for the public to freely visit on weekdays. The alter front has a copy of Leonardo Da Vinci's 'Last Supper' carved in relief and imported from Italy, this was presented to the church by the Morrison-Bell family of Otterburn. It was in this church that the funeral of Evelyn Foster took place, and Evelyn Foster's coffin lay in front of the alter during the funeral service prior to being moved to her final resting place in the churchyard; a black marble headstone resting hard by the church gate marks the final spot. The vicar in 1931 was the Reverend Joseph Philip Basil Brierley, vicar of Otterburn 1919 – 1949. The Rev Brierley also has a place in this story as, not only was he the minister who carried out the service at Evelyn's funeral, he was also a jury member.

Almost directly opposite the church lies another building that played its part that night. This was the Otterburn branch of the Co-Op. The shop which occupied the lower floor, met the grocery needs of the people of Otterburn. Next door to the Co-Op was 'Redesdale', a small house occupied by George Maughan and his wife. It was from 'Redesdale' that the Maughan's set out that night for Otterburn School. On their way they passed a 'strange man' who was walking in the area of the church gate, they were also to pass Evelyn's taxi as it stood outside the 'Kennels' waiting to be filled up with petrol before setting out on its final journey. Little did the Maughan's realise that they would be among the last people to definitely identify Evelyn's taxi before its charred remains was brought back to Otterburn after it had been burned.

George Sinclair was the manager of the Co-Op: he too also saw a 'strange man' loitering near the post office, next door, when he left the Co-Op building that night. George Sinclair would also play his part in the aftermath of what happened that night as he was called to be a jury member at the inquiry hearing. A very important point to note is that from the doors of the Co-Op and its neighbouring cottage, 'Redesdale', there is an uninterrupted view up the road to the 'Kennels' and beyond to the road that leads to Rochester and the Scottish border.

Only a short distance from the church gate, on the same side of the road, stands a large, squat house: stone built it sits at the western end of the village with views to its rear over the Rede Valley. The house stands back from the road which is separated by a garden to the front entered by a central gate, the path then dividing into two and leading to the front two porches for although at one time it was two houses, Joseph Foster had it converted to one. The house was known in those days as the Kennels and it was in the upper left front room of this house, overlooking the main road and the Foster garage beyond, where Evelyn Foster was carried to spend her last hours. Directly opposite the Kennels is a garage: it was from here that

Joseph Foster carried out his business of motor engineer and proprietor of a small bus company.

Evelyn Foster also carried out her business of taxi driving from the same garage although her business was her own and it was only allied to the garage business of her father. In later years a fairground business was run from the garage and today, a coach company is based there. In 1931, the Garage carried a sign: 'The Garage Otterburn' today, the sign has long gone and the garage looks as if it is showing its age. The Foster home also looks bleak today. The house shows little change from the photographs of it in 1931. Even the windows are hung with similar white net curtains, the whole house looking bleak and deserted, which it is.

The village school lies three-quarters of a mile to the west, along the road to Jedburgh, and no one seems to know why the school is built so far from the village or maybe the reason is just lost in time. The schoolhouse was built in the latter part of the nineteenth century by a local entrepreneur named John Davidson. He had also built most of the housing in the village to the west of the Otter Burn. In the early twentieth century the school was certainly to have its share of problems: mainly they were to the result of down-draughting fires that caused the school to be filled with smoke. Water, however, was another problem as the school regularly flooded. The head of the school was regularly to be seen sweeping the water away with a broom. His frustrations and feelings boiled over, however, and he resorted to placing his comments in the school logbook. This action was to place him at odds with the school managers who were forced to discipline the head teacher and a note to this affect reads: '...the logbook is not for the expressions of opinion...the head teacher habitually makes comments and reports criticising the managers...'[1] The researcher today is faced with a number of blacked-out pages in the school logbook of the period, as the managers meticulously blacked out the head teachers comments with black ink and a paint brush.

Within a short distance the road passes Elishaw Road End and is distinctive only in that, this is the point where Deere Street joins the Otterburn to Jedburgh road. Throughout history Elishaw has been variously spelt as, Illeshawe or Illishaugh and its pronunciation is 'Illisha': the name meaning; 'The Wood by The Waters'.[2] The

Umfraville family had a hospital built here: the term here meaning a place for rest and refreshment for travellers rather than the medical term. In its past, Elishaw, was a known meeting place for Gypsies, Tinkers and Pedlars, a place to avoid and stay well clear of. Even today, Elishaw is an uninviting place a bleak road end in the middle of nowhere the road at this point rises and falls as well as twists one way and another; it has the effect of looking and acting like a snake trying to throw the traveller off its back. On the night of 6 January, 1931, Elishaw Road Ends would play a major part in the Evelyn Foster case: a part which has never really been resolved.

It was at Elishaw Road Ends that Evelyn supposedly met the man, the man that she was to give the lift to into Otterburn. This road, which runs south from Elishaw, is the A 68, the original Roman road known as Deere Street that links Corbridge on the River Tyne with Jedburgh, just over the Scottish border. If we are to believe Evelyn's story and that of the people of Otterburn, then this road paid a significant part in the events of 6 January 1931. This is the road on which the car, seen by Evelyn, dropped the man before it drove off down this road on its supposed journey to Hexham.

Like most of the roads in the surrounding area, Deere Street, at this point anyway, is a lonely, meandering road in a bleak, desolate moorland landscape. Some two miles down the road from Elishaw lies Troughend Common on the southern side of Deere Street. A farm occupies this area now however, in 1931, 'Troughend Hall', demolished in 1956, dominated the spot. A further half mile reaches perhaps the bleakest part of Deere Street, a cross roads which leads, to the west, Bellingham and to the east, cuts back into Otterburn where it passes Otterburn Mill on Otterburn's southern end. Bleak and desolate, this area had little public transport; what transport there was, was provided, mainly, by Foster's busses and taxi. This then, was Evelyn's 'patch' as most people who travelled to and from Otterburn relied on her taxi.

After looking at the area involved in the Foster case, the next logical step is to take a look at the other party involved: namely, Evelyn Foster and her family. The census of both 1891 and 1901 shows that John Joseph Foster was born in the Hexham area in 1874, a birth date for him in this year shows that he was born at Haltwhistle near Hexham. His later marriage shows that he was the son of Robert Foster a shepherd. Margaret, Evelyn's mother, was born at Cockle Park, a small farm some four miles to the north of Morpeth. She was the first born child of James and Elizabeth Mary Gordon. Shortly after, James, a farm labourer, made a career change and moved his family to New Hartley where he began work as a miner. Elizabeth Mary Gordon died in 1886 and James remarried in 1894. Joseph's working career began humbly enough as he was employed as a servant, described as a groom, for the vicar of Horsley, Rev Thomas Stephens. Part of his employment allowed him to 'live-in' at the vicarage. How he came to meet Margaret Gordon is unknown as the Delaval area is quite some way from Horsley: some thirty-five miles as the crow flies and not on a normal route. However, the pair married in the Church of *Our Lady* at Delaval on 10 February 1900, the parish church for the Delaval area in which the mining community of New Hartley lies. Margaret is recorded as living in New Hartley while Joseph is recorded as living at neighbouring Hartley [3] where he was employed as a groom.

The first born for the couple was not too long in making an appearance. John Gordon was born to the family at Delaval and duly baptised in the Church of *Our Lady* on 7 June 1900. At this time Joseph was still employed as a groom and this may have been at one of the local mines however, the church register is a bit confusing as it gives the address of both Hartley and Otterburn. It may be that the family were on the point of making a move from Hartley to the Otterburn area. Sure enough, by the census of 1901 taken on 31 March, that year, they were living at High Rochester some four miles to the west of Otterburn. [4] Joseph had taken new employment as a plate-layer on the tramway, probably this was at one of the coal mines in the area as there was no railway station and it may have been an employment change connected to his time in Hartley. The family were soon facing another addition to the family and Evelyn was born on 20 November 1901 her baptism taking place on 5 January 1902 in the *Holy Trinity* Church of Horsley. [5]

It was sometime after Evelyn's birth that Joseph Foster, he seemingly dropped the John from his name apart from official documents, moved his family the short distance from High Rochester to Otterburn. They settled in a large house at the west end of the village known as the 'Kennels'; seemingly the property had supposedly had an association with dogs at an earlier date. [6] Built at the west end of Otterburn, it was the first house at that end. With the severe winds that came over the Cheviot Hills, the 'Kennels' bore the brunt of any storm conditions. To the rear of the house there was a collection of sheds and outbuildings that Joseph Foster put to use as kennels as he had a passion for keeping and breeding Old English Collies.

Joseph's experience working in metal on the tramways was put to good use in the repairing of bicycles and he was soon to set up his own business. Joseph's business began to grow as he carried out repairs on all cycles, motor cycles and motor cars as well as farm tractors and machinery. He now owned the garage across the road from the Kennels and traded under the name of the: 'Otterburn Motor and Cycle Works'. The motor car was still in its 'new-fangled' stage when Joseph Foster began his business in Otterburn and Joseph was at the cutting edge as he was later to write: 'At that time, people believed I was mad. Most of them thought they would get blown to bits if they travelled in a car. Farmers used to laugh at us when we paid £23 for one tyre; they said we could get a horse for as much. Pedestrians would pass us going up hills, then turn round and jeer. Often the cars used to run back on the hills, and to prevent this, we had to put a drag on the wheel. Sometimes, when a car went into a ditch, it had to be taken to pieces to be got back home again. I once had a steam car that would go twenty yards and then stop for twenty minutes.' [7] To enhance his knowledge on the 'new-fangled' motor car, Joseph Foster was to take a course with the Daimler Company in the Midlands.

On his return to Otterburn, Joseph Foster, had the idea of expanding the world for the people of Otterburn. He would open new horizons by transporting locals from their countryside environment to the urban centres of Newcastle and the country town of Hexham. It was from the chassis of an early Daimler car that

Joseph redesigned the bodywork into his first bus of sorts. An early photograph shows two cars, one a Daimler, standing in the garage. Above the garage doors are two notices advertising Singer cycles, one of those singer motor cycles stands between the two parked cars while a couple of pedal cycles stand against the wall to the left. A uniformed driver sits in each of the cars: a dark haired man stands between the motor cycle and one of the motor cars. Of dark appearance and with a dark moustache, this man is Joseph Foster.

Of more interest is the car to the left, in the back seat sits a woman who, with her rounded face appearance, looks as if it could be Margaret Foster. To her front, in the front passenger seat of the car sits a young girl of around three or four years old. The face is rounded and there is a decisive gap in the centre of her hairline in all probability this is Evelyn Foster making one of her early associations with the motor car. The addition of Evelyn Foster would date the photograph to around 1904/05. After a gap of eight years, Dorothy Edith was born on 17 June 1909 followed by Margaret Elizabeth baptised 10 December 1911. The Foster family was now complete: they were to be a close-knit family in a village known, like most other rural, Northumbrian communities, for its close-knit community spirit.

Evelyn, like the rest of the Foster children, was to attend the local school however; she appears to have left no mark on the school. The school logbook fails to mention her at all apart from one brief note that records that Margaret Foster sent a note to the school informing the head teacher that Evelyn had stayed away from school for one day. When Evelyn left Otterburn School her future employment was secured as she began work in her father's garage business. Mostly, at first, this was to be the serving of petrol from the petrol pumps outside the 'Kennels'. Joseph Foster's business had begun to expand as he provided a service for local people to travel to Newcastle and Hexham.

However, it was with the First World War that Joseph's business came into its own. From 1911, the British Army had been using the Otterburn ranges for training purposes: they had one shortcoming for the Army; there was no transport for their heavy equipment to and from the local railway stations. These stations were at Knowesgate and Woodburn and, while the Army could get their heavy equipment from the south of the country to either of these stations, they could get it no further. Enter Joseph Foster; he had invested in some heavy trucks and he transported the Army equipment to and from Knowesgate and Woodburn Stations. In between these transporting trips, Joseph Foster had found another niche that he filled and exploited: the transporting of heavy farming equipment, to and from these same stations to any of the farms in the area.

With the end of hostilities, there was still a need for the transport of Army equipment. However, Joseph Foster saw another niche yet to be filled. Although he had initially provided a small service for locals, carrying them here and there, there was a need for a proper bus service. Much of the country was on the move by public transport, why not Otterburn? There was only himself to provide a service within Otterburn: between Otterburn and Newcastle there was no competition in public transport: to meet this end Joseph Foster invested in a bus. That Joseph Foster's passenger bus service was a success, is reflected in the fact, that, shortly after the end of the First World War, he owned a fleet of ten busses,

mostly of the Albion make. It was also during this period, mainly due to the fact that many men were returning home from the war, that there was a surplice of men with no, or few, jobs to accommodate them. Joseph Foster's garage and bus business supplied work for a few men who were willing to travel away from their home area: for these men there was also accommodation at the bothy. The Foster busses could now supply a full bus service between Otterburn and Newcastle as well as Hexham. In later years his daughters would work on the busses as conductresses, mainly filling in for regular staff.

In appearance, Evelyn Foster, mainly took after her mother. Her post mortem report shows that she stood at around five feet and weighed in at around ten and a half stones; her general appearance tended towards a rather dumpy physique. However, she was also known to be quite pretty without being over attractive and is still remembered in that way by the older residents of Otterburn. Her face was of broad appearance topped with fair hair tending towards the 'mousey' colour. Photographs during this period give the impression that her hair was dark, leading many reports to describe her as brunette. Her hairline also had a distinctive gap, just off centre which tended to be disguised by the fact that it ran into the centre parting of her hair; her hair on one side sloping down to disguise the gap. In a portrait photograph, her hair is brushed back which accentuates the gap in her hairline. Her hair, although tending to the longish, she always wore in an 'up' style and she regularly wore it in plaits, one each side of the head, the plaits were then wound around her ears in a style which came to be known as the 'headphones' or 'earphones' as they looked like headphones worn by the female telephone operators of the day. This style was also given, in the American slang of the day as, 'Cootie Garages.' In style, it was a common hair style throughout the nineteen twenties, in particular among those known as 'flappers.'

A family portrait shows that her arms look solid and tends to accentuate her 'dumpiness'. To overcome this somewhat, Evelyn, tended to wear loose fitting clothes that hung on her frame rather than clinging to it in an effort to disguise her figure. A photograph taken of her around the late twenties shows her standing next to her taxi. This car is an Essex, a similar model to the Hudson Super Six she was later to have. It shows a happy, smiling Evelyn Foster dressed in her work or taxi-driving clothes. She wears a long, heavy overcoat, a necessity in cars with no heaters, which hangs down to her mid leg. Beneath this she wears heavy, woollen long socks, probably from the nearby Otterburn Woollen Mill and a sensible pair of lace-up shoes. She wears a dark coloured 'cloche' hat, fashionable headwear for women of the twenties and this was in all probability, if not the hat she wore on her final night of 6 January 1931 then a one very similar to it. Overall she has the appearance of being a woman in fashion without being over the top.

Evelyn Foster learned to drive at an early age, probably shortly after leaving school if not before; there was no driving test in those days. It is known that she was allowed to drive the locals around on short taxing trips and, in time, she built up her own clientele. She appeared to have a very cheerful personality, always ready to sit and enjoy the local gossip, and people would increasingly ask for her driving services personally. She was at this time also manning the petrol pumps as well as filling in as a conductress on the busses. After suffering a short illness, her father bought her a 'tin lizzie' Ford as she had been informed by the Doctor that she needed more fresh air.

Seemingly it was at this point that Joseph Foster turned the taxi side of his business over to Evelyn. Although Evelyn Foster is mostly thought of as a taxi driver, self employed, and nothing else, this is not altogether true. According to the evidence of Joseph Foster, at the hearing of February, 1931, Evelyn was responsible for carrying out secretarial work for the Foster business, garage and all motoring administration, as well as serving petrol when needed and standing in on the busses, although these duties were increasingly passed on to her sisters: she also had general housework to do. To suggest she was merely a taxi driver is a bit of an understatement of her workload.

EVELYN AND HER ESSEX CAR

Originally, Joseph Foster had carried out all the local taxi duties in and around Otterburn. Mostly this was to help his friends but it was also used as a courtesy to his customers. As his family grew up, it was Gordon Foster who took over the taxi driving between his duties at the garage. As the bus business expanded it slowly overhauled the use of the taxi, mainly on the longer routes. When Evelyn became of age to drive, she took over the taxi driving although, mainly on the shorter routes and even then only in the daylight hours. As with the buses, there was little competition within the taxi business and, as getting around by taxi had become much more popular, the Foster taxi business was pushed more onto Evelyn and then handed over to her solely. It was also known that Evelyn was prone to giving the local children a ride in the taxi or even a day out for a picnic in the surrounding countryside. As the taxi business grew, Evelyn took possession of a successive number of increasingly larger cars, mostly of American origin. Among the cars she owned was a Buick followed in turn by an Essex. The Essex was a similar car in both size and shape to her final car, the Hudson Super Six; the Hudson and the Essex motor cars were built in Detroit and exported to the UK.

Women driving cars, and in particular driving hire cars, were not so common in the UK prior to 1914. However, with the commencement of hostilities in 1914, driving cars as an occupation became much more accessible to women. The men were taken away for the services leaving the women behind to carry out their duties. With the cessation of hostilities in 1918, women were reluctant to give up their new-found freedom and use to the workforce. In the rural areas of Northumberland this was even more common than in the urban areas. Women had just won the right to vote, for women aged thirty and over, from 1918, for women aged twenty-one, that was to come in 1928: they certainly were not going to give up their rights to work.

In the area around Otterburn, there were three women driving hire cars as a profession. Apart from Evelyn, there was Miss Brannan who ran a hire car from the 'Bird In The Bush' Inn at nearby Elsdon. Her hire car was mainly for the use of transporting locals as well clientele to and from the Inn. Mary Glass was in a similar situation as she drove a hire car as part of her duties at 'The Railway Inn' in Bellingham, her father was the landlord. The Inn had formerly run horses and traps for hire: the First World War saw the horses and traps replaced by a motor car complete with a driver. The driver was to stay only long enough, before Army service, to teach Mary Glass to drive the car and Mary Glass took over the driving duties. Part of her duties was to chauffeur local businessmen around the area and she visited Otterburn, on average, around twice a week. As a driver, she naturally patronised the Foster garage and came to know Evelyn quite well.

As the taxi business expanded its workload, Evelyn became increasingly in demand. People were not only needing transport to convey them from shopping locally, they were becoming more socially aware and visiting local meetings and parties as well as dances. The majority of these people needed the services of Evelyn's taxi to get them home again. Joseph Foster's original idea of bringing the town to the countryside had the additional effect of increasing the range of Evelyn's taxi. Local people no longer wished to stay in Otterburn for their entertainment; they wanted a night at the theatre in Newcastle. The current bus schedules did not fit in with the timings of these shows so, Evelyn found her taxi service more and more in demand for trips to Newcastle. Among her local duties, she was called upon to chauffeur various ministers to their churches throughout the district.

In the rural areas of Northumberland and especially near the Scottish border, many ministers were called upon to preach at more than one church: in particular among the non conformist religions of which

EVELYN FOSTER AT THE KENNELS

Presbyterianism was one, the Scottish religion spreading across the border as many Scots people moved into the northern counties in search of work. One of Evelyn's 'regulars' was the local Presbyterian minister who preached at Byrness hard by the Scottish border. Although Byrness was a small village, its population had exploded with the increase of navvies and their families, during the building of the Catcleugh Reservoir between 1899 and 1905; the 'Klondike' conditions meant that many of the shanty dwellings remained for many years as did many of the families. Another local community was the Redesdale Army camp near Rochester, many of the Army stragglers were to rely on Evelyn's taxi to get them back to camp.

When Evelyn took over the taxi side of the business, the cars that she drove were purchased at her own expense. All the regular servicing and maintenance of the car was to be carried out by the Foster garage; all petrol was from the petrol pumps outside the 'Kennels' and was noted in a notebook carried by Evelyn. All costs were then paid at the end of a month. The road tax on the car as well as the hackney licence was paid for by Evelyn. Although the insurance on the car was paid for by Evelyn it was covered by two policies, floating policies, they were under the name of her father and the business, according to Joseph Foster; this was because they were at a cheaper rate that way. One policy was to cover the car while it was on the garage premises; the other was to cover the car while it was on the road against any accident, with or without other vehicles. Much of the work in the hire car business was carried out by use of the telephone as well as the leaving of messages; the garage was also used for this purpose. However, it is also known that messages involving the use of the hire car could be left at various other points. One of these points was certainly the 'Percy Arms' and she may have used other public establishments as well.

Evelyn appeared to be a normal, maybe shy, person who seemed to be liked by everyone who knew her. She appeared to have a normal social life and was a regular attendee at the village dances at the 'War Memorial Hall'. It was during one of these dances that she met Ernest Primrose, a Scotsman and former soldier, who was employed by Joseph Foster as a bus driver. In time the friendship evolved to the point where many thought the Evelyn and Ernest Primrose would be married. For some reason the relationship did not endure the course of time and it is thought that Evelyn brought an end to the relationship.

Even at work, Evelyn had found herself often standing in as a conductress when Ernest Primrose was driving the bus from either

Newcastle or Hexham. All of this came to an end when Evelyn brought an end to the relationship to the extent that shifts were changed to avoid Evelyn sharing the same bus as Ernest Primrose. Perhaps this caused embarrassment to Ernest Primrose, as all of the Foster employees were aware of the friendship. Not long after, Ernest handed in his notice to Joseph Foster and departed north to his native Leith. Evelyn appeared to have no difficulty in entering another relationship: in a short period she had begun a friendship with George Philipson, a joiner at the Foster garage.

It is known that both Ernest Primrose and George Philipson had both been regular visitors to the 'Kennels', mainly for dinner during their respective friendships with Evelyn Foster. This must have been something special as even today older residents of Otterburn, remember that the Foster's, as a family, were difficult to get to know. They would speak to anyone but that's as far as it got and they were sociable only up to a point; not many were granted permission to enter the inner sanctum of the Foster household. They were known to be of the village but apart from it; what was their business remained that way and outsiders were not part of the Foster household.

It may be worthy of note that, just as Ernest Primrose had terminated his employment with the Foster's, after the break in the relationship with Evelyn; George Philipson appeared to do likewise. Not long after the death of Evelyn Foster, George Philipson had moved from the bothy and was living within Otterburn Tower; presumably to live there he would also to have had to have been an employee as it was not a hotel or a place that had bed and breakfast facilities. Evelyn must have been in her mid twenties when she had begun the relationship with Ernest Primrose: perhaps the Foster's as parents were a little too strict on Evelyn's relationships. It is worthy of note also: when Evelyn was brought back to her home, after the events at Wolf's Nick, the first name mentioned, as to who could have been responsible for the fire, was Ernest Primrose.

NOTES.

1) Otterburn School Logbooks. Northumberland Archives Woodhorn.

2) Rev J. Hodgson. 'History of Northumberland Part 11 Vol 1. Frank Graham Reprint. 1973.

3) The twin mining communities of Hartley and New Hartley lie in the area of Delaval in 1862 they hit the headlines when they suffered one of the worst mining disasters in history. A beam snapped and fell down the shaft, blocking it and 204 men were entombed and suffocated to death.

4) The 1901 census: this has the wrong age for Joseph Foster, knocking two years off his age. His year of birth is given as 1876, in actual fact, it was 1874.

5) The birth of Evelyn on 20 November1901 makes her age 29 and not 28 as so often reported. It also makes here headstone wrong as her age recorded there is 28 years. Oddly, her age in the coroner's report, is also recorded as 28.

6) Although the Kennels may have had associations with dogs at some period in its past when the Foster's moved there, 1902/03, the Kennels had been used as a grocers shop of sorts. This had been a grocers shop since at least 1881 and used as such by Isabella Swanston. In the census of 1871 and 1861 the Kennels was the home of George Robinson, a Carrier, with Isabella Swanston as his servant/housekeeper. Presumably she took the house over as a shop sometime between 1871 and 1881. In the census of 1861 and 1851 the house bore no name at all. In 1911, the Kennels was still two cottages, a family called Jennings lived in the other cottage.

7) Goodman P 16.

CHAPTER TWO

THE STORY.

The story begins with the Foster family of Otterburn. Joseph Foster, the father, ran a garage at the west end of Otterburn village. Over the years from 1901, Joseph Foster had built up the business from a small, bicycle repair workshop into a motor vehicle repair business: this was housed in a garage opposite the 'Kennels'. He was later to add a few busses to his business and began to provide a regular bus service to Newcastle and Hexham. In addition to the busses, he also owned one or two cars; these were to provide an extension of his bus service as well as aiding locals who lived away from the bus service routes. Petrol was also needed for the running of the transport and petrol pumps were added outside the 'Kennels' providing another small extension to the Foster business; the selling of petrol. The garage then became a meeting point for those from the area with cars. Over the years, the addition of heavy vehicles, to provide transport for the Army to and from the Army camp at Redesdale and the nearby railway stations at Woodburn and Knowesgate meant that the Foster business was rivalled in size only by the Waddell family business that ran Otterburn Mill. Although transport was still in its infancy and Otterburn was out in the wilds, a second garage was in Otterburn. This was run by Thomas Gibson and situated opposite the

'Percy Arms'. However, it appears to have only lasted between the years 1922 to 1928.

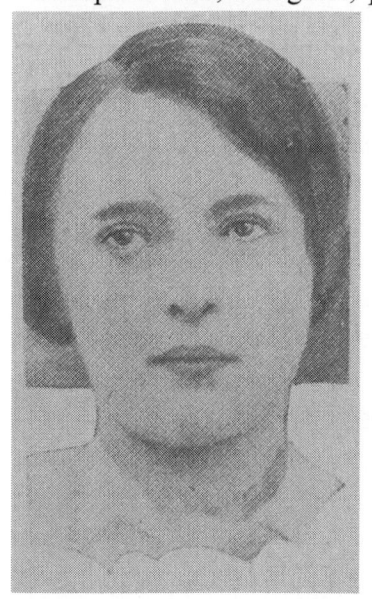

Joseph's wife, Margaret, provided the office expertise as well as running the family home. A number of men were employed to drive the various vehicles as well as working in the garage, most of these originating from outside Otterburn: the population was none too large and most of the locals were employed in farming. However, following the First World War, employment generally began to slump as the result of cutbacks mainly in the large industries as their output, geared to the war effort was now on the wane. Lack of employment along with social unrest brought about the General Strike of 1926. Men were now more prepared as well as forced by lack of employment, to seek work in other parts of the Country. Many 'outsiders', therefore, drifted into Otterburn, some of them finding employment with the Foster's. Many of these men resided in the bothy. Along with employment, the living accommodation gave the men incentive to take pride in their work as; to lose their employment also meant losing their home.

The build up to the First World War and its continuation from 1914 through to 1918, was to maintain added pressure on the Foster business and more so on the car hire side of the business. In reality the demand on the taxi business, started only as a measure of goodwill to the locals, was becoming increasingly heavy due to the ferrying of the increasing number of soldiers to the Redesdale Army Camp from the nearby station at Knowesgate. The Army made further demands on the Foster business in the use of the Foster's heavy transport vehicles for towing their guns, again from Knowesgate to the Army camp. Evelyn had learned to drive while still at school, there were no official tests in those days, and by the age of fifteen was driving her fathers' taxi around the district on short journeys, mainly for people who were known to the Fosters.

Evelyn soon progressed, on leaving school, to full time employment with the Foster business. She would help with work on the petrol pumps as well as stand- in work as a conductress on the busses and, when needed, could be seen driving the taxi.

In the early twenties, Evelyn was working almost full time on the car hire side of the business and was soon to build up her own regulars. Evelyn appeared to have some trauma with the dentist, having gone through some dental surgery; she became 'run down'. As part of her treatment, she was advised to spend more time in the fresh air. It was around this time that her father bought her a 'tin lizzie' Ford and Evelyn began to take more customers spending more time driving around the countryside. With Evelyn taking on more responsibility in the business and the garage business taking up more and more time of both Joseph and Gordon, the car hire business was handed over to Evelyn in name if not deed.

Although the car hire business was in conjunction with the garage business it was autonomous. The car would be kept in the garage and maintained there as well as being insured through the garage insurance, apart from that however, the day-to-day running of the taxi was carried out by Evelyn. Although she would seek advice on aspects of the running of it, such as pricing fares: this was to happen on the night of 6 January1931. In the late 1920s early 1930s, the thought of a woman running a car hire business seems a little too advanced. However, a car hire business was run from the 'Bird In The Bush Inn' at nearby Elsdon and was run by a Miss Brannen while other young women were also to drive cars during this period, mainly because they had been taught to during the war so that they could take over the duties of male drivers.

So that she could accommodate more passengers in reasonable comfort, Evelyn had mostly bought cars of the larger variety after parting with her original 'tin lizzie' Ford. Large cars also meant foreign cars and, in Evelyn's case this meant American cars. In a few short years, Evelyn had invested in a number of American cars. She had owned a Buick, a Dodge an Overland and an Essex. Her latest acquisition was a Hudson Super Six bought the year before in 1930. This car had been purchased from Rossleigh and Co in Newcastle for the sum of £200. Like her other cars, it was second hand but, at two years old it was not seen as an old car.

To make the most of the bus service, as well as providing more service for the locals, the bus service terminated at Otterburn but passengers from farms and other outlying places further up Redesdale would be taken on to their destination by Evelyn's taxi: in effect an extension of the bus service. The nature of the service provided by Evelyn demanded that she work seven days a week as well as the odd late night. Evelyn's taxi provided a service that took people home from late night dances and other social occasions normally held at, among other places, the War Memorial Hall. Evelyn also provided transport for those who wished a night out in Newcastle; places like the Theatre Royal or even the cinema were popular venues as well as being still a novelty in those days.

The events of 6 January 1931 began just before 6-30 pm with the arrival in Otterburn of the regular service bus from Hexham. In the driver's seat was Cecil Johnstone who pulled the bus into the forecourt of the 'Percy Arms'. Mainly this was to allow the passengers to disembark but also to allow the conductor, Tommy Rutherford, to deliver some newspapers that had been picked up at Hexham. When the bus proceeded up the main street to the Foster garage, the final stop, there were still three passengers aboard; two male passengers were going on to Rochester while the third a woman, Mrs Esther Murray, was going on to Cottonhopeburn Foot. With the two male passengers dropped off at Rochester, Evelyn agreed to take Mrs Murray on to Birdhopecraig Hall. Mainly this was because the night was so cold but it also allowed Evelyn the advantage of using the Hall entrance to turn her taxi. The pair sat talking for a few minutes and, as they did so, a car was seen to pass travelling from the direction of Jedburgh; the sight of another car on the road at that time was sufficiently rare to warrant the attention of the two.

Evelyn, after leaving Mrs Murray, began her journey back to Otterburn. On approaching a point called Elishaw Road Ends, Evelyn noted a car parked there and a man came across the road and began to flag her down. The man explained that he had missed the Edinburgh to Newcastle bus at Jedburgh he then stated that he had met the people in the car, sitting in the car across the road, and had tea with them. The people then gave him a lift to Elishaw where, it was thought, after a short walk or, better still, a lift, he could catch a bus from Otterburn to Newcastle. The people in the car, he told Evelyn, were going on to Hexham. Evelyn informed the man that the bus had already left Otterburn for Newcastle however, she would give him a lift into the village and he could see if he could get a lift from there to Ponteland where the man could get a bus to take him on to Newcastle.

While in the car for the short drive to Otterburn, Evelyn and the man had come to some agreement; she would take him into Otterburn the man could then ask in the village about a lift to either Ponteland or Newcastle. If the man was unsuccessful Evelyn would then pick the man up at the bridge and take him on to Ponteland. Evelyn had stopped the car outside the 'Kennels' and went into the house. As for the man, presumably, he got out and walked the short distance to the 'Percy Arms' to make enquiries about a lift.

While in the house, Evelyn had conveyed the story to her mother and asked her father about a price for the fare to Newcastle. Her mother, naturally, was more interested in the man and asked what he was like to which Evelyn stated that he was: 'Very respectable and gentlemanly like....he looks a bit of a nut.' Evelyn stated that she already told the man that the fare would be around £2. Her mother thought that this was a bit on the high side and on telling her daughter, Evelyn was to make the reply: 'Get daddy to work it out while I'm filling the car.'[1] After filling the car with petrol Evelyn returned to the house where her father informed her that the fare should be £1-16-0. By this time Evelyn's sister, Margaret had arrived on the scene and, after gaining the gist of the story suggested that Evelyn should take along George Philipson, a friend of Evelyn's. This Evelyn assured her she would do and, taking a torch departed from the house.

The truth about what happened next, as far as Evelyn is concerned, is mainly down to conjecture and the statement by Evelyn conveyed to the Police by her mother. It would appear the mystery man could not get a lift in Otterburn and he met up with Evelyn once more at the bridge next to the 'Percy Arms'. They then departed in a south-easterly direction out of Otterburn towards their destination, Ponteland. However, they never arrived: in fact they only appeared to get as far as Belsay. It was here that the man was to have second thoughts for, according to Evelyn, he no longer wanted to go to

Ponteland but wished now to return to Otterburn. On their way back to Otterburn, the man made it clear he wanted to drive the car and on refusing him, Evelyn was punched in the face. The car seemingly travelled on, presumably with the man driving, as far as Wolf's Nick where for some reason it was stopped. The man seemingly now forced Evelyn into the back seat of the car, possibly attacking her again after which something from a bottle was thrown over Evelyn.[2] The car was then set in motion and it careered over the verge on the right side of the road, plunging down an embankment and onto the moor over which it travelled some distance before it was halted by a ditch. Either at this time or before it left the road, the car was set on fire with Evelyn still in the back seat.

Shortly after 9 pm the last bus from Newcastle to Otterburn left the Haymarket bust station, Newcastle. At the wheel was Cecil Johnstone and his conductor was Tommy Rutherford who shared the bus with a handful of passengers: none going as far as Otterburn. As the bus travelled the road to Otterburn, north of Belsay, only the two Foster employees were aboard. Soon after this, Cecil Johnstone stopped the bus and changed places with Tommy Rutherford. The purpose of this was to allow Tommy Rutherford a little bit of unofficial driving practice while no passengers were aboard. Therefore, as the bus passed through the gap that was Wolf's Nick it was Tommy Rutherford who was at the wheel. With Tommy Rutherford's eyes concentrating on the road ahead, it was Cecil Johnstone who first caught site of the glow of a fire on the moors off to the right. After some short debate as to what it was, the bus was brought to a halt. Cecil Johnstone was first to alight, Tommy Rutherford electing to stay with the bus at first.

As Johnstone approached the fire he concluded that the source of the fire was a car. Thinking that someone may still be in the vehicle, Johnston hurried towards the car and, in the light of the fire, read the number plate as TN 8135: a number that he was familiar with as it was Evelyn Foster's Hudson. At this time, Johnstone had been joined by Rutherford and, after a brief look round, the two decided that there was no one in the car however, a slight moaning could be heard somewhere near the front of the car. A further look round and Tommy Rutherford noticed something black lying between the car and the road. On approach, Tommy Rutherford recognised the object as being Evelyn Foster.

It must have been a shocking sight for the pair. Evelyn lay on her side, her head turned even further away and her whole body moving in a rhythmic motion the cause of this being that Evelyn, her thirst brought on by the fire, was licking the ice lying on the moor in an effort to quench her thirst. Her body was naked from the waist down and even her shoes had vanished. Where the clothes met the flesh of her body, the two had fused together forming odd stumps that passed for her limbs. The air all round was filled with the rancid smell of burned flesh which forced the stomach of the two men to their very limits. Cecil Johnstone immediately took off his overcoat and wrapped it round the body of Evelyn. Her left hand, he noticed, was gripped tightly around some bracken probably in an effort to aid some movement. Cecil Johnstone pulled her hand away and folded her arm so that it fitted into the coat as he did so he noticed that her palm was almost burnt away.

Leaning over Evelyn, Cecil Johnstone could not see the full extent of her injuries on her face only noticing that her eyes were puffed up and swollen resembling only slits. He had, however, seen enough of her injuries to know that she was suffering from severe burns. Cecil Johnstone told Evelyn who he was but did not see even the merest flicker of any recognition. Taking a further quick look around in case there was anyone else who may have been a passenger: Cecil Johnstone could see no one, he then realised this was no time for further questioning and told Evelyn he was taking her home. Evelyn was to reply: 'If only you can help me stand I could walk to the bus'. Without hesitation Cecil Johnstone picked Evelyn up and began to walk back to the bus, Tommy Rutherford in front to guide the way and to open the door of the bus. Once inside, Evelyn was placed on a seat and the bus set off at full speed for Otterburn.

The moon had waned by now and the moors were returned to their covering of darkness. However, as much as the road conditions would allow, Cecil Johnstone drove his bus back towards Otterburn as fast as it would go stopping only at a farm to get water to quench Evelyn's thirst, the bus arrived in Otterburn at 10-30 pm. Cecil Johnstone first sought out Gordon Foster and he, Joseph Foster and Dorothy Foster went into the bus. Thomas Vasey, a motor mechanic at the Foster garage, had been working in the garage, on hearing the bus arrive, Vasey, entered the bus: there he saw that Evelyn, was propped up on a seat and although terribly burned she was still fully conscious. Recognising Vasey, Evelyn said: 'Oh Vasey lift me up.' Vasey then asked Evelyn who had done this to which Evelyn was to reply: 'He threw something over me and set fire to me and the car'. Evelyn was then carried by Vasey and Johnstone up to her room, above the front room of the house, and laid on her bed which had been hastily prepared. Cecil Johnstone was then sent to Elsdon to pick up District Nurse Lawson while telephone calls were made to the Police and the Doctor.

Evelyn had been sitting inside the car, on the rear seat. All that she could remember was that after the man had thrown something over her she was set alight remembering only that car was 'bump bumping' as if travelling over rough ground. There then appears to be a gap of who knows how long, before she found herself lying outside the car: how she got there she could not remember. After she had gained consciousness, she could not remember how long she had been in that state; she heard the sound of a car stopping followed by a whistle. Her immediate thoughts were that, the attacker had been hailed by an accomplice and driven away from the scene of the crime in a car. However, the theory was soon dashed when Walter Smith Beattie came forward a few days later. After reading of the event in a newspaper, it was he, he said, who passed Wolf's Nick at that time.

Walter Smith Beattie, a motor salesman for Croal and Bryson's in Hawick, just across the border, had picked up a car in Darlington and was on his way back to Hawick. Passing Wolf's Nick, he had seen a burning car within thirty or forty yards of the road. He stated that there was: 'Smoke and small flames around the body of the car which he recognised as a saloon, the flames were not high'. He could see no one in the vicinity and came to the conclusion that the car had just been left there. Judging by the state of the fire he estimated that it had been burning for about thirty minutes. He then drove off as he felt there was nothing that he could do. Walter Smith Beattie could not remember at what time he passed Wolf's Nick. He did however, make the same journey five days later and noted his times and speed, from this he deduced that he had passed Wolf's Nick at around 9-50 pm.

The District Nurse, after viewing the wounds, found that all she could really do was treat Evelyn's facial burns, the rest was beyond her and Evelyn needed strong drugs in order to combat the pain. The local police were soon in action. Constable Fergusson, after being alerted by Joseph Foster at 10-45 pm, made a telephone call to Sgt Shanks at Bellingham Police Station at 10-50 pm. Sgt Shanks then made contact with Dr McEachran and the two drove across to Otterburn, arriving there at 11-30 pm. On duty at this time in Bellingham was Constable Henry Proud. Making his rounds, Constable Proud, noticed a car with its lights on standing outside Dr Miller's house, on enquiring if anything was wrong, Dr Miller relayed the story of Evelyn Foster as best he knew it and informed him that he needed a driver as he had an injured foot. Constable Proud, killing two birds with one stone, volunteered his services and the two drove to Otterburn arriving there at around 12-00 pm.

Dr Miller went straight into the Kennels while Constable Proud enquired at the Garage about the Police presence. He was told that Constable Fergusson was at the Police House, Constable Proud made his way there, the Police house was sited near Otterburn Mill. Constable's Fergusson and Proud then made their way to the Foster Garage where they joined up with Sgt Shanks. On arrival at the Garage, they found Joseph Foster heating oil; this was to put in a car that would take the Police officers out to Wolf's Nick in order to examine the crime scene. So far the Police had not entered the 'Kennels' and it would appear that they felt no emergency to question Evelyn. All of this changed on being informed that she may not last much longer.

On entering the room where Evelyn lay, the Police were to note that there were six people in the room, District Nurse Lawson, Margaret Foster, the two Doctors and themselves; it would appear that Constable Proud had been left in the Garage. Sgt Shanks directed Constable Fergusson to take down the notes as Margaret Foster passed questions between the two. This odd behaviour resulted in Constable Fergusson asking questions, Margret Foster asking the same questions of Evelyn then passing on the answers. Goodman stated that Constable Fergusson was having difficulty hearing what Evelyn was saying, this being the reason that Margaret Foster asked the questions. In fact, Evelyn's voice seemed to be understood by all who were in the room. Dr McEachran, while still treating Evelyn, was also listening to the to and fro of the questioning and he was to later state on one point: 'While lying on the fell she heard the petrol tank explode. I have no doubt about this last statement.'[3]

The rest of the questioning appears to have gone off without any incident, the Police officers returning to the Garage across the road. The car that Joseph Foster had prepared was now ready to convey the Police to Wolf's Nick, the scene of the crime. Thomas Vasey, a mechanic, was to drive the car and was to give the Hudson a quick look-over; this was expressly on the orders of Gordon Foster. This was to see if the car was in gear or not. Cecil Johnstone was to accompany him and guide him to the exact spot. The car left Otterburn around 12-40 am and proceeded to Wolf's Nick arriving there at around 1 am. Precisely what the Police hoped to find on an open moor in the dark is not recorded; however, there was now an official Police presence at the crime scene.

It appeared that no one really knew what they were looking for at Wolf's Nick. Both drivers and Police appeared to be engrossed in doing their own thing. Cecil Johnstone and Thomas Vasey occupied themselves by looking around the car, inside and out, with no apparent thought about touching anything. Thomas Vasey checked to see if the car was in or out of gear; Constable Proud heard Vasey say: 'This car's in gear'. On approaching the car, Thomas Vasey was to note that: 'The rear tyres were smouldering and the rest of the car was burned out.' On looking inside the car as well as looking under the bonnet he was moved to state: I formed the opinion that the fire had started there (inside the car) as the engine was not burned at all severely'.

Thomas Vasey had also come across a petrol can; this he described as standing on its 'narrow' side and with the handle burned off, he also saw Constable Proud pick up a scarf and what appeared to be a piece of suspender from near the back of the car. Constable Proud was later to deny finding any piece of suspender in his statement. Cecil Johnstone, his mind on what Evelyn had said, was looking for a bottle or a tin but, found neither. He did state, however, that both offside doors were open and the others closed. He did not say if this was the way that they were left after he and Tommy Rutherford had left the crime scene. Constable Proud was also to note that the rear tyres of the Hudson were smouldering while no other part of the car was burning and the two offside doors were in the open position. At the rear of the car, Constable Proud, found a piece of material that turned out to be a scarf, he placed it back where he found it saying, seemingly to anyone that was listening, 'I'll leave it where it is'.

At this point, someone thought to carry out a wider search of the surrounding area and Constable Fergusson and Sgt Shanks departed leaving Cecil Johnstone and Thomas Vasey wandering around the moor; Constable Proud was left to stand guard on the car. The two policemen went first to Kirkwhelpington Police station to inform Constable Francis Sinton of the occurrence at Wolf's Nick. It was while they were at Kirkwhelpington that the Police examined the contents of a purse, found by Constable Proud, at the scene. This was found to contain: two ten shilling notes, 9/6 in silver (under 50p in today's currency), two driving licences in the name of Evelyn Foster, one expired and one current. They then moved on to Mr Charlton's farm at Reedchester where they made a search of the outbuildings before returning once more to Wolf's Nick. After picking up the others from Wolf's Nick, they moved on to Ottercops Farm where, farmer Mr Telfer informed them that he had returned from Scotsgap at 8 pm and had seen nothing out of the ordinary. The group now made their way back towards Otterburn. They made searches at one or two farms along the way searching their outhouses and barns with no success. The last stop they were to make was, ironically, that last place Evelyn's Hudson had been positively identified; Raylees Farm. Farmer, Mr John Armstrong was to report that nothing and been seen or heard and the search revealed likewise. The car then set off once more and carried on to Otterburn. Still not fully satisfied, the Police carried out a search in the immediate vicinity of Otterburn, a search that once again revealed nothing. Constable Proud then made the return journey to Bellingham with Dr Miller arriving there at 5 am.

The next Policeman to make an appearance was Inspector Edward Russell from Prudhoe; some twenty-five miles to the south, on the river Tyne. Russell had been alerted by the Hexham office. On his way to Otterburn, Inspector Russell, stopped at Ridsdale at 5-50 am, and gave the story, as he knew it, to Constable William Turnbull, a copy of the original telephone message to Hexham, regarding the occurrence at Wolf's Nick, was also shown to Constable Turnbull. Russell, as senior Police Officer, then instructed Constable Turnbull to proceed to Wolf's Nick and take charge of the burned car. Constable Turnbull was the only Policeman so far with his own motorised transport, a motor cycle. He travelled to Wolf's Nick and took up his duties as from 6-30 am. He was immediately struck by the fact that he was the only person there and he was to state: 'I did not go near the car as I was not aware what the investigations of the early morning had disclosed in the form of footprints.' At around this time the local populace was beginning to make their way to work. Robert Pringle, was on his way to work at Knowesgate quarry, at 7 am he was pushing his cycle up the steep hill to Wolf's Nick: when he stopped and enquired of Constable Turnbull, who was stamping his feet against the early morning cold, what was going on, he received only the frosty reply: 'move along' which he did without further question.

Inspector Edward Russell proceeded from Ridsdale to Otterburn where he arrived at the Garage at 6-05 am. Asking if he could speak to Evelyn he was informed that she was unconscious. Inspector Russell then went to the Police house to be given all the information. He then returned to the Kennels at 9-15 am where he hoped to question Evelyn. He was informed by Joseph Foster that his daughter had died at 8-55 am. Since being questioned by the Police, Evelyn had been in and out of consciousness for increasingly longer periods as she neared death. Making a final revelation or a final attempt at a statement she turned her head in her mother's direction and said, in an almost whisper: 'Mother....I have been murdered.'

It was later that day that Inspector Russell travelled to Wolf's Nick in company with Constable Fergusson: with the help of Constable Turnbull, they carried out a detailed survey of the crime scene. Inspector Russell walked and measured the final route made by the Hudson as it had made its last journey over the moorland, finally coming to a halt some eighty-four feet south of telegraph pole number 636. Russell came across a two-gallon Shell petrol can: 'standing on its bottom on the offside of the steel platform of the car: the neck was lying on the nearside some six inches away.' Russell was also to go to state that: 'None of the grass or heather, over which the car had travelled was burned.' The car said Russell: 'Had been burned where it stood.' Russell also came across the scarf worn by Evelyn, picked up by Constable Proud it was now draped over the nearside headlight of the Hudson. The two offside doors were still in the open position and the other two were closed.

The newspapers were soon on the job looking for a good story, they soon found that all the ingredients were there. A girl taxi driver, going about her business, murdered on a lonely moor. The murder, evidently, carried out by a strong man, a man who had then drifted away into the mists of the moors, was now at large somewhere on those same moors. The moors were also part of the story and much emphasis was placed on the small hills known as the Ottercops, to the north of the scene of the crime. Most editions of the newspapers carried large format photographs of the stricken, burned-out Hudson. These adorned the pages along with a portrait photograph of Evelyn Foster and presented the story to the public. Headlines such as: 'Wolf's Nick Tragedy', 'Murder On The Ottercops', 'Alleged Fiendish Attack On Girl' and 'Stunned Then Fired' were soon grabbing at the attention of a public not only in Northumberland but, throughout the Country. It was newspaper headlines such as these, along with their reports, that thrust Otterburn onto the pages of the national press and into the minds of the population. Otterburn, a quiet village most of the time, had to face an influx of newspaper reporters in their midst searching for the latest headline.

Otterburn Village became the hub of activity over the next few days. Inspector Russell, investigating the Hudson at Wolf's Nick, asked Gordon Foster, to provide a lorry to remove the Hudson from the moor. Gordon Foster had to move the gear into neutral to allow the car to be moved, restoring it into low gear under the inspection of Inspector Russell. The Hudson was removed to Otterburn, from where it had departed the night the before, and placed under lock and key in the Foster garage, where it was to await the inspection of a motor expert.

The expert picked to carry out the inspection was William Jennings, a motor engineer who ran a business from Bridge Street in Morpeth. Looking over the car, Jennings, found that the matting on the running boards was more scorched towards the rear of the car than the front. The engine, although scorched, showed no real signs of severe fire at all. In fact the front of the car, although scorched, was not badly burned and even the registration plate was intact. The fire, he noted, had begun within the rear of the car.

Moving to the back of the car, Jennings was to note that the ends of the springs, that supported the petrol tank, had suffered so much from the intense heat that they had bent, under the weight of the petrol tank, turning down some four inches. All the soldered joints on the petrol tank had given way to the intense heat and melted, even the drain plug on the bottom of the petrol tank had fallen away yet, the filler cap, was still firmly in position. Perhaps more amazing, the petrol tank still held its full contents. One of the statements made by Evelyn and heard by Dr McEachran, was that the petrol tank had exploded. She had heard it go off.

Jennings was satisfied that nothing mechanical had caused the fire and stated, to the press: 'That some agency outside of the car itself had been the cause of the fire but whether inflammable liquid or other material has been the medium, there is no evidence on the car to show.' Jennings was to elaborate further when called on to give his description of the fire: 'I am of the opinion that the fire commenced within or at the rear of the body. The flames have spread in an upward and forward direction.' According to William Jennings therefore, the fire had nothing to do with the running of the car: the fire was caused by someone deliberately setting the car alight and, although he could not prove by what means, the fire had started within or around the rear of the Hudson. Although subject to intense heat which had almost destroyed everything around the back of the car, the petrol tank had failed to ignite.

Joseph Foster was interviewed by the police on the details of Evelyn's Hudson. He was to state that, the Hudson Super Six had been bought fourteen months previous by Evelyn from Rossleigh's in Newcastle. Evelyn had paid for the car herself and it had cost her just over £200. In order to reduce the costs on insurance, the car had been insured through her father's company, the car was insured for £450. Evelyn was not rich but she could support herself and, he went on to reveal, she had £487-4-8 in the bank with a further £8-4-0 in her Post Office account.[4] Joseph Foster had no idea about the incomings and outgoings of her taxi business, this, he said, was all written down in a book. As to the whereabouts of this book: it was, he said, kept in a compartment within her car.

Although the case had set out strongly in favour of Evelyn Foster, all the reports had pointed to a particularly nasty murder of a poor girl; things were to change as the days went on with no result. The police were convinced that they would apprehend the murderer, whether alive or dead, he could not evade them forever, there were far too many clues. One of these clues that the police placed much faith in was the finding of the car that had dropped the stranger at Elishaw Road Ends, as well as the woman driver. Nothing, however, was forthcoming and doubts were beginning to form in the ranks of the police fuelled by reports in the press.

Allied to the missing woman in the car, was the increasing doubt over the existence of the missing man. To add even further doubt was the inspection of the Hudson. This was to show that the car, far from being set alight on the road, as Evelyn had stated, had been set alight where it stood on the moor. Evidence showed that the car had been set alight from inside the rear of the car: in reality this was to show that the car could have been set on fire either by the man or, by Evelyn herself, either way it fanned the flames of doubt. As for the insurance, it was now stated by Joseph Foster that the car was insured for twice as much as Evelyn had paid for it. All little things on their own, however, when laid side by side they added up to one large, increasing doubt.

So incensed was Joseph Foster, with the accident theory instigated by William Jennings report, now appearing in the press, he gave his own statements to the press in defence of his daughter. This was carried out by giving the special correspondent of the *Evening World*, a guided tour as he examined the Hudson in the garage. Joseph Foster was quoted as saying: 'To say that the fire was an accident is an insult to the intelligence.' He pointed out at this point, that he also was a motor engineering expert, the quote being directed towards William Jennings. He then went on to say: 'The murder was a well planned plot' and, 'must have been done by a man who must have known about the petrol tin (kept in an unlocked box at the back of the car) and must have known the roads.' All of this made good reading but bore little resemblance to fact, and, in reality, only showed that this was a defence of a daughter by her father. A 'well planned plot' would have to at least have had a motive. There was no robbery involved, the car was not stolen, just wrecked and Evelyn Foster had lost her life, apparently without motive or gain.

The centre of attention now moved away from individuals to the main street of Otterburn. Slightly east of the Church, and standing on the opposite side of the street, sits the Village 'War Memorial Hall': a small building that carried the names of the dead of Otterburn who fell in the First World War. The hall was used for a variety of events associated with village social life such as various meetings, parties and dances. Evelyn had driven many people home from these events in the 'War Memorial Hall' and, just over a week previously she had attended the Christmas festivities there. That same War Memorial Hall, still carrying the Christmas decorations, was to be the centre of an inquest into her death. The inquest was merely a formal affair mainly to give the proof of identity of the deceased and lay the foundation, as well as setting a date, for the future inquest. The Coroner was to be Philip Mark Dodds, Coroner for the south district of Northumberland.

A jury of nine people was soon set up. All of them were from Otterburn Village and all were so well known to the court officer, Constable Fergusson that he reeled their names off as they were called without even looking at his book where the names were written. Joseph Foster was called as the first witness under his full name of John Joseph Foster. The *Newcastle Journal* was to describe the scene to its readers, Mr Foster: 'Suffering under great emotion, and sank into the chair offered him by Coroner P.M. Dodds. He struggled to give his name and that he was the father of the deceased. The reporter from the *Newcastle Journal* noticing that; 'Now and again he wiped his brow and covered his eyes.' Bringing the short inquest to an end, the Coroner now adjourned the inquest until 2 February and proceeded to inform the jury that this was: 'A formal fixing because we may not have to meet if proceedings intervene.' Joseph Foster, along with son Gordon, left the 'War Memorial Hall' by the back door, probably with the intention of avoiding the press which had gathered; they were photographed by a press photographer as they left.

The landscape had been frosty and ice covered on the night of the events of 6 January. Snow had also fallen during the last few days however, on Sunday, 11 January, Redesdale and Otterburn were enshrouded in mist and rain as the day dawned for the funeral of Evelyn Foster. If Otterburn had been busy so far it was to become even more so on this day. According to the local reports, people had travelled from all the towns and villages for miles around. From Newcastle to Alnwick and from Morpeth to Jedburgh, they literally  arrived in their hundreds and descended on Otterburn. Of course, not all were true mourners and many were of the sight-seeing variety, their only reason for being there would be the fact that they were in Otterburn on the day that Evelyn Foster was buried. Mourners were to arrive by many differing means of transport, causing increased difficulty for the police with many walking for miles over the mist-shrouded moors and fells just to get there. Working on the theory that a murderer returns to the scene of the crime, some policemen were dressed in everyday clothes as they mixed with the mourners hoping to catch the man who had so far eluded them.

At around 2 pm, the funeral procession began its journey from the 'Kennels', a mere hundred yards, to the Church of *St John the Evangelist*. Evelyn's coffin was borne by four Foster employees followed by the immediate family and friends who were followed in turn by mourners as many as eight to ten deep as they walked down the street. Awaiting their arrival at the church gate was Rev J.P.B Brierley, who would carry out the service, accompanied by Rev F.N. Wright, vicar of Horsley. The church was soon filled to bursting point with many forming outside the church listening to the strains of the organ played by schoolmistress Miss Ferry and the congregation singing 'Rock of Ages' as many outside were seen to openly sob. As the coffin was born outside once more the rain began to come down heavy, even so, all men were seen to be bareheaded and, with the last part of the graveside service there seemed to be a palatable silence. Only after the grave was filled with the coffin of Evelyn and the last of the flowers laid, did Margaret Foster allow herself to be led away. The *Newcastle Journal* was to report: 'The funeral yesterday was one of the saddest ceremonies but even in the midst of their grief the parents and relatives of the dead girl must have found some little solace in the great outgoing of sympathy from their own folk of the villages and dales.'

The funeral and opening of the inquest was over and nothing now remained but the formal part of the inquest. The village now looked forward to some peace. The press on the other hand, needed more news and one part of the story would not rest in peace; the man was still somewhere and every stranger, it seemed, was likely to be *the* strange man. A man was seen near the gates of the church, a man who fitted the description given by Evelyn. He approached two youths, they told the Special Correspondent of *The Evening World*, and asked where he might get a lift to Newcastle. They were to note that he had a Tyneside accent, however, before they could answer footsteps were heard and the man said: 'Is that a policeman coming.' He then vanished into the darkness up the Rochester road. A mystery man was also seen by a boy riding a bicycle. The boy rode towards the man in order to get a better look. The man then yelled: 'What are you taking notice of me for', interspersed with a number of oaths. The boy was badly scared according to *The Evening World* and took off while the man once more disappeared into the darkness and was seen no more.

NOTES.

1) Evelyn Foster in the statement given by her mother. Coroner's Report COS/3/54/1. Northumberland Archives.

2) There was rumours that some corrosive, thought to be vitriol, was thrown over Evelyn, either from a bottle or tin that the man carried in his pocket: first stated by Evelyn in her statement: this was picked up by the press and denied by the police.

3) Statement by Dr McEachran. Coroner's Report.

4) Jonathan Goodman. The Burning Of Evelyn Foster; P 102. Notes that Evelyn was worth £1,442 gross in two banks, she was only with one according to Joseph Foster. He also states that if the insurance were to pay out on the burned car Evelyn would only receive a total of £45.

CHAPTER THREE

A POLICE PRESENCE.

Although, reading through the small amount that has so far been published on the Evelyn Foster case, we could be forgiven for thinking that the police were not present. If they were, then they were not much good, was the general consensus, and this is the sad tale that has been handed down through time. A tale tainted with incompetence and fanned by press coverage in pursuit of a story as opposed to truth and, at any cost. There had in effect, been a police presence since the beginning of the Foster case. This was of course, in the shape of Constable Andrew Fergusson, the local village 'Bobby'. His home and office were combined in the police house near the Otterburn Mill on the Bellingham to Otterburn road. The majority of Constable Fergusson's duties, as with any other rural village policeman, centred around the village and district peacekeeping which, in most cases was drunkenness, fighting and the occasional poaching offence. On the night of 6 January 1931, all that was to change as his ordinary life was turned into the extraordinary. Constable Fergusson was highlighted in a possible murder case and thrust into the media spotlight by a press, local and national, hoping to get the scoop on the murder.

At around 10-45 pm, Joseph Foster, made a telephone call to Constable Fergusson to report that his daughter and her car, had been burned and left on the Ottercops at a place known as Wolf's Nick. Constable Fergusson then informed his immediate superior, Sergeant Robert Shanks, at Bellingham police station, making a call within five minutes of being informed of the events, informing him of the occurrence at Wolf's Nick. Constable Fergusson then made his way to the Foster garage, about a quarter of a mile away on the other side of the village. There is no information on the reason why he arrived at the garage rather than the Kennels, it may have been that the garage was where Joseph Foster was and that he wanted to get the facts, putting off a visit to Evelyn Foster until the arrival of Sgt Shanks.

It would appear that Constable Fergusson may have been in the garage on his own as it was Thomas Vasey who first alerted Joseph and Gordon Foster to his presence. Constable Fergusson then spoke to the pair for a while, allowing them to convey the story as they knew it. Having just picked up the pieces themselves, it would not be much. According to Goodman, it was at this point that Joseph Foster asked Constable Fergusson if he had initiated a search for the man yet. This, if it was true, appears to be a bit previous at the least as there had been no confirmation of the man's description yet. Neither was it up to Constable Fergusson to initiate any kind of search even if he had known what the man looked like.

Very few police officers in the area had any form of motorised transport during this period. Constable Sinton at Redesdale was one of the few, but he was not yet in the story. Sergeant Shanks certainly had no transport and he was alerted by Dr McEachran of Bellingham, who drove the two of them to Otterburn: the pair arriving at Otterburn garage at 11-30 pm, Dr McEachran going straight to the 'Kennels' while Sergeant Shanks went to the garage. He was quickly given a resume of the story by Constable Fergusson prior to speaking to Joseph and Gordon Foster. It was clear by now that more police, higher up the chain of command, should be alerted to the occurrence of that night. To this end, Sergeant Shanks sent

Constable Fergusson to inform Superintendent Thomas Shell of Hexham Division, the division in which Otterburn lay.

At this point, it has been stated, that there was a bit of a fracas involving Constable Fergusson and Joseph Foster. [1] This involved the use of Foster's telephone rather than walking all the way back to the police house. In reality, both Sergeant Shanks and Constable Fergusson returned to the police house and the fracas, in actual fact did not happen. It is more than possible that this was one of the stories, passed on by word of mouth, which has now been passed into folklore as fact in the Evelyn Foster case. It is normal for police business to be carried out on a police telephone; there may well have been other things of note that the two policemen would have had to hand in the police house.

Over at Bellingham, Constable Henry Proud was on duty and making his rounds of the village when he noticed a car, with its lights on, standing outside the house of Dr Miller at 11-25 pm. No doubt thinking that he could be of assistance in some way, Constable Proud approached the Doctor to enquire if anything was wrong. Dr Miller informed him of the occurrence at Wolf's Nick involving Evelyn Foster. He was to further state that he was in need of a driver as he had injured his foot. Constable Proud attempted to inform Sergeant Shanks but was told that he was already in attendance at Otterburn. Seemingly Sergeant Shanks had tried to get in touch with Constable Proud but failed as the latter was somewhere out on his beat. After dropping off Dr Miller at the 'Kennels', Constable Proud walked across to the garage to enquire about the police presence and, on being told that Fergusson and Shanks were at the police house, Constable Proud made his way down to meet them.

It was while in the garage, according to Goodman, that Gordon Foster informed the police that he had instructed Thomas Vasey to take a car out to Wolf' Nick and, if they wished, they were welcome to accompany him. However, according to Constable Proud, it was when the police returned to the garage; 'Joseph Foster was heating oil to put in a car to take them to Wolf's Nick,' a somewhat different perspective. However, it cannot be denied that there was a definite 'them and us' attitude developing between the police and the Fosters, later to gain substance by incorporating the people of Otterburn; a feeling that was to last for many years, perhaps even into the present day. That the feeling had a valid cause is a matter of opinion, however, it existed.

The Police were informed by Dr McEachran that if they wished to ask questions of Evelyn Foster they better do so as death was imminent. With this, Sergeant Shanks and Constable Fergusson entered the Kennels and were confronted, for the first time, with the badly burned Evelyn Foster. Also in the room was the district nurse, Nurse Lawson, the two Doctors and Margaret Foster. There would appear to have been very little organisation over who was to interview Evelyn, in effect, it was Constable Furgusson who would take notes while Margaret Foster would ask the questions and pass on the answers. As Sergeant Shanks was the more senior officer present it would have been natural to think that he should have carried out the questioning. In effect, Constable Furgusson was to state on returning to the garage: 'I commenced to take a statement from Evelyn, her mother was asking the questions and I was making the notes.' Who made the decision is not clear as nothing was recorded. The apparent difficulty Fergusson had, with hearing what Evelyn said, and recorded by one writer [2] just did not happen. This appears, more than likely, to have been passed by word of mouth and handed down through the ages as fact, in order to reflect as incompetence by the police and that they were just not up to the job in hand.

With the interview of Evelyn Foster over, the police had now to begin to search the area beginning with the scene of the crime at Wolf's Nick. The police were driven there by Thomas Vasey in one of the Foster cars. Cecil Johnstone made the trip as well however; his reason for doing so appears to be a little vague. Gordon Foster had sent Thomas Vasey, not only to drive the car, but also to check if the Hudson was in gear. In order to have checked this, Thomas Vasey, would have had to touch the Hudson, something which he surely should not have been allowed to do and, Constable Fergusson warned him not to interfere with anything. As for Cecil Johnstone; all he seems to have done was walk around the moor in the vicinity of the car. As the police were later to be looking for footprints this was not the best thing to be doing at that time.

Constable Proud came across a piece of material which he picked up and decided that it was a scarf. He returned it to where he had picked it up with the words: 'I will leave it here where it is', for the benefit of who the words were for, Constable Proud did not say. However, Thomas Vasey appears to have been nearby and stated the Constable Proud picked up pieces of what appeared to be a woman's suspender. Constable Proud was later to make it quite clear in a statement: 'Whilst at the car at Wolf's Nick I did not pick up anything which resembled in any way a lady's suspender. At this time, it was noted that two offside doors of the Hudson were open and those on the nearside were closed this was noticed by the police as well as Cecil Johnstone; they also noticed that, although the Hudson was no longer burning they tyres were smouldering.[3]

Sergeant Shanks, after a cursory look around, decided to widen the search area and took Constable Furgusson with him in the Foster car. In the meantime, Constable Proud came across an object, in the vicinity of the rear of the car that turned out to be Evelyn's purse. He just caught Shanks and Furgusson before they departed and handed it over to them. The crime scene was now left under the watch of Constable Proud. However, also left at the scene were Cecil Johnstone and Thomas Vasey, free to wander over the area. A question at this time would appear to be; how much of the ground was trampled around the car and, more important, how much of the car had been touched? Thomas Vasey had found the petrol tin and had also been inside the car, to test if the car was in gear but, also, he had been under the bonnet of the car looking at the engine even though Constable Fergusson had warned him not to interfere with anything. Sergeant Shanks and Constable Fergusson drove to Kirkwhelpington to inform Constable Sinton of the occurrence at Wolf's Nick. After a search around some of the local farms in the area, Shanks and Fergusson returned to Wolf's Nick to pick up the others and departed around 4 am. There is now a gap from 4 am to 6-30 am when the Hudson, and the crime scene, was left completely unguarded.

After receiving the telephone call from Constable Fergusson, Hexham division then alerted Inspector Edward Russell at Prudhoe as well as Northumberland County Constabulary HQ at Morpeth. Inspector Russell then set off on his journey north stopping off at Ridsdale, on the Hexham road south of West Woodburn, to inform Constable William Turnbull of the occurrence at Wolf's Nick.

Russell then told Turnbull to proceed to Wolf's Nick and take guard of the car; Constable Turnbull arrived at Wolf's Nick on his motorcycle at 6-30 am. The Hudson had stood unguarded for some two and a half hours, Constable Turnbull noting that he was the only person at Wolf's Nick. Inspector Russell now carried on his journey to Otterburn where he hoped to interview Evelyn Foster, unfortunately, on his arrival at the garage; he was informed by Joseph Foster that his daughter was unconscious. Inspector Russell busied himself around the immediate area of Otterburn in an attempt to put the story into perspective. He then returned later, to the 'Kennels' at around 9-15 am hoping to interview Evelyn; however, he was out of luck again being informed by Joseph Foster that his daughter had died at 8-55 am.

Inspector Russell was the first senior police officer to visit the area. Later that afternoon, he became the first senior officer to visit the actual scene of the crime and make any detailed measurements and observations. He was to note that the tyre marks were still visible on the road as well as down the banking; a track he followed and measured, all 198 feet of it, from source to ending. He, like others before him, noticed the petrol tin; 'Standing on its bottom on the offside of the steel platform' at the rear of the car.' Only a matter of fifteen hours before, Thomas Vasey, had noted that this petrol tin was standing on: 'Its narrow side.' The petrol tin had obviously been moved at some stage. There was also the anomaly of the moving doors. Cecil Johnstone and later, Constables Fergusson and Proud had noted that two offside doors were in the open position on their visit to Wolf's Nick. Inspector Russell, arriving at 3-30 pm, was also to notice that the two offside doors were open and none others. Goodman was to state that the doors were in various positions of openness during Wednesday; indicating that someone else had been to Wolf's Nick. [4]

Inspector Russell also spotted blood traces on the nearside door handle as well as the nearside mudguard these, along with some blood on the ground some twelve feet from the front wheel of the car, were all preserved for further investigation. On looking around the car Inspector Russell, found that the worst of the fire damage had been contained inside the rear of the car and, after walking along the track of the car with no sign of any burning to the heather or scrub, he came to the conclusion that: 'The car had been burned where it stood.' Russell also picked up various items, mainly cloth, from the nearside from of the car. A scarf was hanging on the nearside headlight of the car: it should be noted that Constable Proud had picked up the scarf on his earlier visit and had made a point of returning it. One report, in more recent times, laid blame on the press of the day.[5] However, the car had been under constant guard since 6-30 am and no press had visited Wolf's Nick before that time. The perpetrator, if there was one, must have come from the police themselves or either Thomas Vasey or Cecil Johnstone: failing this, someone must have walked past the policeman on duty and tampered with the evidence.

The Northumberland force may have lacked a CID unit however, in the Foster case the discrepancy was more than adequately filled by Inspector Russell. As we have seen, he was the first police officer to systematically cover the crime scene at Wolf's Nick. No one else had so far even measured out the various distances covered by the car. He also searched the area picking up pieces here and there, mainly pieces of cloth that had been worn by Evelyn Foster, the scarf and a piece of charred material in the shape of a cone, thought to be Evelyn's hat, all were collected and sent off to the College of Medicines at Newcastle for close examination by Professor McDonald. He was also to supervise the removal of the burned Hudson from the moor, making sure that Gordon Foster returned the gear lever back to low gear, the way that he had found it. Later, Inspector Russell was to inspect the interior of the car more closely; he was to find the remains of a pocket flash lamp, presumably the one taken from the 'Kennels' by Evelyn and, more importantly: 'The burned remains of a book under the skeleton of the driver's seat.' This was all that remained of Evelyn's account book, now charred and passed reading.

Two main points were to rankle the local press, bringing any amount of discord with the relations with the police, from the very outset. The full report of what had happened at Wolf's Nick had been passed on to only two newspapers, the *North Mail* and, oddly, the *Sporting Man*. The *Newcastle Evening Chronicle* was stung into action to mention this fact on 7 January, while sister publication, the *Newcastle Daily Journal* was to retaliate the following day: 'The police have a difficult task. It might have been less difficult had the newspapers been notified immediately of the crime, so that a description of the passenger in Miss Foster's car could have been circulated right throughout Northumberland and further afield. What a curious thing it is that if the police desire a dead body to be identified they will notify the press immediately, but if it is a live body, urgently wanted for some horrible crime, they are not so quick to seek the aid of the most efficient publicity medium.' Clearly the police were not to be the flavour of the day in local press circles.

It was also the local press who began probably the worst slur against the Northumberland force that they were likely to come against, calling for Scotland Yard to be called in to carry out any investigation into the crime, a crime that was not yet a day old yet, the press were giving the impression that they had lost confidence in the police. This was probably the worst statement that could be aimed at the police during this period. In turn this brought forth a statement from Northumberland County Constabulary on 8 January: 'Scotland Yard has definitely not been called in said a high official at Northumberland Police Headquarters at Morpeth.' The suggestion he added was apparently because of the broadcast message last night. This 'message' had to go through the Metropolitan Police, but that is all, they had nothing to do with it.' The broadcast referred to was the description of the wanted man in connection with the Foster case. The passing on of information, on the BBC, had to be passed through the official channels, in this case the Metropolitan Police. The *Newcastle Evening Chronicle* was not to take much notice of this and continued to lead with the headline: 'Will Yard be called in moor murder.'

In 1931 there were not a great number of policemen in the County of Northumberland, just over three-hundred. Even those were widely spread over the County, the fifth largest in the Country. Many of the larger villages had their local 'Bobby' who was trained, and expected, to act as the local peacemaker. Mainly their duty was to manage the local drunks or petty crimes rather than any serious crime. A larger police presence was to be found in the towns such Hexham, Morpeth, Alnwick and Gosforth; Newcastle had its own separate police force. Transport, for the largest majority of the rural policemen was the pedal cycle. Although a cycle got the policeman mobile in order to cover a wider district, in areas such as Otterburn, getting around on a cycle was both time consuming and hard work. Motorised transport was very limited in the Northumberland force: one of the few to have a motor cycle was Constable Francis Sinton of Ridsdale: first to be placed on guard of the car at Wolf's Nick.

Various police constables were to be on duty at Wolf's Nick during the day following the events of 6 January During the day of 7 January there was also a large press presence and, judging from the photographs of the period, an equally large presence of VIP sightseers who appeared to feel the need to be there without any real purpose. All appeared to be there with the blessing of the police. This was irrespective of the damage they were doing to the surface of the moor regarding footprints that may have been left by any assailant. Following this up two days later with: "The Evening Chronicle was informed today by Scotland Yard that no special request has been sent by the Northumberland Police to them for assistance with the Otterburn case." Asked if Chief Inspector Helby and Sergeant Bell (Scotland Yard detectives) were holding themselves in readiness to leave for the north at any moment an official of the Yard said: "Scotland yard is taking no part in the investigations. If that were the case we would have been called in long before now." Eventually this was to become a long-running saga that was to outlast the Foster case itself; so long-running that it can even be detected today some eighty years after the occurrence at Wolf's Nick.

The Chief Constable of Northumberland County Constabulary was based at Morpeth, some fifteen miles to the east of Wolf's Nick. During this period, the Chief Constable was Captain Fullarton James, an Irish-born ex Army officer. Fullarton James had been born in Dublin, 1865, the fifth son of East-West Indian Merchant, Francis E. James and his Scots born wife, Helen D, James. Francis and Helen James had a family of ten and, judging by their various places of birth the family had moved around considerably. Although most of his family were born in Dublin, as Francis had also been, the family had also lived in Wales and various parts of England. The 1881 census shows that the family at that time lived at number 50, Lancaster Gate, Paddington.

Although mainly Irish there was a Scottish influence in the family, apart from their Scottish born mother, three of their staff also came from Ayr, birthplace of their mother. Fullarton James had served in the British Army and was to carry his rank of captain into the police service when he was appointed Chief Constable of Radnor in Wales, in 1897. He was to be appointed Chief Constable of Northumberland as from July 1900. Fullarton James had no official police training and was granted the post of Chief Constable purely on account that he was a former Army officer with good family connections. It is interesting to note that, many officers in the British Army, during the late Victorian period and before, were also granted commissions in the Army based mainly on the fact that they had good family connections: that, and more than a little money with which to purchase their commission. Fullarton James was to receive the Police Medal, June, 1916 and was awarded the CBE, presumably for length of service, in 1925.

Captain Fullarton James had taken up the post of Chief Constable in July 1900; at that time the Northumberland force was still in the throes of the Victorian period. During his time with the Northumberland force, Fullarton James, was to keep the Northumberland County Constabulary within the confines of the Victorian period, in effect, he kept it in a sort of time warp. The force was to receive no motorised transport until 1930, even then it was limited, and was not to have a trained CID department until after he left in 1935. However, as we shall see, it did have some kind of limited detective force working in it during early 1931. Fullarton James was known to have taken part in one or two murder cases among them the Morpeth train murder of 1910. During his time as Chief Constable of Northumberland he was to have more than a few brushes with the Home Office.

OTTERBURN TOWERS TODAY

A bane of contention during the Foster case was to be the lack of trained detectives. In a force of over three-hundred police officers there were no CID officers within the Northumberland police force. Much emphasis, on this lack of CID as well as any trained detectives, has been placed by various writers on the Foster case. [6] There were, it seems, three plain-clothes officers who were merely police constables that were not required to wear uniform. However, one fact of the Foster case was, that an officer who was taking statements during this period, was John Eckford; he took the statement of Mary Murray, passenger of Evelyn Foster's taxi. John Eckford was to sign that statement not only with his name but, the addition of 'Detective No 7'. It can safely be assumed, therefore, that there were some detectives on the Northumberland force at this time. Presumably, going off the signed statement taken by John Eckford, at least seven of them: where or which station they were attached to is not stated. It is doubtful if these officers were seconded from any other force, to help the Northumberland force, as Fullarton James seemed to be against such moves.

INSP RUSSELL - SUPT SPRATT ON THE MOOR

When the Foster case opened, it carried all the hallmarks of a murder investigation. It was decided, therefore, to open an incident room in Otterburn. To this end Otterburn Tower was chosen to be the local Otterburn headquarters. Otterburn Tower had been owned by the late Howard Pease, a local antiquarian, who had died three years earlier. Otterburn Tower was, at that time, in the care of his wife, Margaret Pease. During this period all statements from the police were on notepaper with the heading: Otterburn Tower. The lower ranks of the police were involved in the taking of the many statements from people who thought they had something that could be of help. Many of the witnesses had to be visited a second time as they had additions to make to their original statements or wished to clarify certain points. Many of these statements were not to be used in the eventual hearing for various reasons. For the upper ranks, their emphasis was placed mainly on evaluation of the statements and evidence. On occasion they could be seen at Wolf's Nick as they went over the measurements of the moorland where the car had travelled and where it eventually came to rest.

During the first few days there was much movement around Otterburn and its area by the police, whether interviewing or searching. However, it was some ten days before it was decided to dig up the moorland at Wolf's Nick where the car had stood and where Evelyn Foster had been found. During this period the weather had changed from hard frost, at the time of the occurrence to rain-sodden bog due to a thaw and heavy rain. Both Superintendent Spratt and Inspector Russell were photographed during this period digging up the moorland. Supt Spratt, with what appears to be a king-size spade. Naturally the local press were present to report the scene: 'Working with great precision Superintendent Spratt searched each sod as it was lifted. Here and there he picked out a small stone and other objects and carefully wrapped these in pieces of newspaper.' The reporter appeared a bit piqued when he noted that there was a natural reticence from the officers who refused to discuss their actions and failed to make any statements about the case at all.

However, the report was to continue: 'After three hours of work, during which they were soaked to the skin by the heavy rain, the police officers removed over eight square yards of turf. The boxes containing this were afterwards conveyed by lorry to Otterburn Tower, the mansion which serves as headquarters for the police engaged on this case. Later today they will be examined by detectives, who will be aided by experts.' Of interest is that fact that the reporter seemed to think there were detectives involved in the case. Most of the evidence found by Inspector Russell on a previous visit, had been passed on to the College of Medicines at Newcastle, there it came under the charge of Professor McDonald. All of the turf dug up on this day however, was only to prove, according to Inspector Russell: 'That there was nothing of importance apart from a hairpin.' Apart from Evelyn Foster's dying statement, there was no evidence of a man at all. If however, it could be proved without doubt that there was more than one make of petrol in the turf then the police would be in the possession of substantial proof that someone else had been involved and Evelyn's statement would be deemed valid. No different traces of petrol were found. The turf was then presumably dumped again.

There was much enthusiasm during the first few days after the occurrence at Wolf's Nick. The police were much in evidence as they searched the local farms and various buildings in and around Otterburn, the press hanging on to their every word hoping for the inevitable 'scoop'. The police were, the press announced, confident of an early arrest as there were so many clues for them to go on. There was increased activity in Otterburn with police motor cycles coming and going as well as much activity in and around Otterburn Tower; newspaper headlines such as a: 'Great hue and cry throughout the whole area' gave an air of police being highly active. The description of the 'much-wanted man' was soon to be circulated with added emphasis being placed on the driver of the car that had brought him to the area of Elishaw Road Ends. It was hailed by the press as: 'The most dramatic man-hunt Northumberland had ever seen.' This was followed up by the local press reporting on various stories, on a daily basis, covered by the local police: not all based on fact.

TROUGHEND HALL

It was during this early period, that reports of the incident at Wolf's Nick were circulated to other police stations throughout the area. Mainly, it has to be said, in the belief that the man may have escaped the immediate search area but could still be on the loose within the County of Northumberland. Acting on nothing else but the statement of Evelyn Foster, police officers were sent to Jedburgh to interview anyone that may have information. Jedburgh is a small Scottish border town; even so, it is hard to understand where the police would start in an attempt to interview anyone. The man had merely said that he had taken tea with friends, it could have been a cafe, pub or even a private house, even so, there were a number of likely establishments in Jedburgh. Of course there is also the fact that the man may have lied to Evelyn in the first place. The police officers also stopped off at Rochester, just west of Otterburn, to interview the landlord of the 'Redesdale Arms', Ben Prior. One writer was to give a description of Ben Prior as a: '...cantankerous but interesting ancient codger who, when fuelled with sufficient whiskey, could tell a riveting tale about nothing in particular.'[7] He had only seen three strangers that night, in a group, and they left in an Essex; a car similar to Evelyn's, and departed in the direction of Otterburn.

On their travels, in and around Otterburn, the police were to question many people. Among the more outlying places visited was Troughend, a farming community with a manor house, Troughend Hall, standing in its own grounds. This was the residence of a couple named Clark, the woman only identified by Goodman as Mrs 'X.'[8] However, no one appears to have been available at the time of the police visit and no reference was made as to whether the police made a return visit or not. It was from around this period that the attitude of the police was to change.

Newspaper reports began to question if there really was a man on one hand and, on the other they began to question the ability of the police. As we have already seen, the press began to question if, or when, Scotland Yard should become involved in the investigation. Also surfacing were queries, mainly within the ranks of the police but also within press circles, as to the authenticity of Evelyn's statement. No witnesses had come forward to state that they had seen a strange man, as detailed in Evelyn's statement. After an appeal by the police, no one had come forward to validate Evelyn's claim that there was a car at Elishaw Road End that night: the car that supposedly had carried the strange man from Jedburgh. With so much doubt surrounding the case the police hardly needed more.

However, more doubt was to be cast on the case as early as 14 January, a mere eight days after the incident. The first inquiry hearing was to be held in the 'War Memorial Hall' on the Thursday: much of the hearing was to be a mere formality however; all attention was focused on one witness, the pathologist, Professor McDonald. He was to confirm that he had found no marks of violence whatever on Evelyn: there was no visible signs of any punching, slapping or any other form of attack to back up the story that Evelyn had stated. The following day the press were to highlight the story with the *Newcastle Evening Chronicle* headlining 'Two conflicting reports.' In one they noted there was the statement of Evelyn Foster stating that she had received a blow to the face with a fist; in the other was the report by Prof McDonald that stated that there was no sign of violence whatever. If there had been doubts in the ranks of the police before, they certainly had grounds for more now. While the evidence could be seen as coming down on the side of the police it was suggested that the evidence created a wider chasm between the police and the people of Otterburn.

With the first hearing over and adjourned until 2 February, the Foster case bogged down with only elements of the press keeping it alive with often dubious stories. These mainly cantered on sightings of the strange man, in many parts of the County and even further afield. Anyone with a bowler hat had become an instant suspect and, closer to Otterburn; anyone at all who was a stranger immediately became a suspect and was reported to the police. While it kept the newspapers occupied with stories it also had the effect of tying the police down with useless searches, most of which were fruitless. The more that was written about the man being still on the loose the more it served to foster even more fear among the people of the area, especially those who lived in the more remote areas of the County. In turn this led to more supposed sightings and tended to tie-up the police even more.

New evidence was continually coming to light, especially as the Foster case began to bog down, the press made every effort to keep the story alive. One piece of new evidence was the acid theory. This theory was founded mainly on the fact that Evelyn had stated that the man, had taken a bottle or tin from his pocket and thrown the contents over her. This evidence was apparently backed up by both Cecil Johnstone and Joseph Foster. The *Newcastle Evening Chronicle* was to state: 'A startling new theory that vitriol was thrown over Miss Evelyn Foster before she met her death on the lonely Otterburn moorlands now confronts the police, who confess themselves baffled by the extraordinary turns which events have taken. The coat in which Mr Cecil Johnstone, the bus driver, wrapped Miss Foster when he found her dying beside the burning car shows signs of having been burnt with acid. Then Mr Foster, Evelyn's father, told me that the blankets on the bed into which the dying girl was put when she was brought home were similarly burnt.' Seemingly this piece of evidence was only released to the press and not the police: a common occurrence in the Foster case. The police were soon to stamp out any idea of this theory when they released, to the press, that the story was: 'All wrong: we have had no information whatever about corrosive acid.' It would appear from this little exchange that, the case was turning into almost, a trial by the press. It was not to last however, as the story appears to have died a death and no further evidence on corrosive acid was to be put forward.

Probably the most noteworthy, if not headline-grabbing incident so far, in the run-up to the inquiry hearing, was proposed by Joseph Foster. His dissatisfaction with the police handling of the case, allied with lack of results, caused him frustration and he proposed to the police that he should offer a reward: 'Even though it may ruin his business.' However, his offer was refused by the police. All this did was to further increase Joseph Foster's frustrations and, in the eyes of the public at least, added more frustration and lack of confidence in the police handling of the case. With the opening of the inquiry hearing on 2 February, those in favour of Evelyn Foster's innocence were to receive two set-backs. The hearing was informed that they were faced with only two choices; murder or accident, suicide was to be ruled out completely. If that statement had been bad, worse was to follow. The Coroner also ruled that Evelyn's statement would be heard only on the proviso that it was not taken as 'evidence of fact' but merely used as a guideline to the inquiry; Evelyn was to be guilty until proven innocent. At the end of the hearing the press were quick to launch their view with the headlines noting that, at least, there had been a clash of wills. The *Evening World* was an example with: 'Police disagree with jury.' Once more there was a call for Scotland Yard's assistance; once more there was a denial.

In the aftermath of the hearing it was thought that things could just not get any worse, they did. It was to be revealed that Chief Constable Fullarton James had seemingly given an interview to one of the national newspapers. In the interview he was to be quoted as saying that neither the man, nor the woman in the car at Elishaw who had given him the lift, existed; at least outside the head of Evelyn Foster. He was further to state; Evelyn had started the fire herself. Naturally this was to receive full coverage of the press who went on to enquire if the Chief Constable had made such a statement. This led, of course, to a denial. However, the damage had been well and truly done. Joseph Foster was to see the statement by Fullarton James as nothing short of a personal attack against the integrity of his daughter. Claim and counter claim was made and Joseph Foster finally made it clear that he would write to his MP.

The verdict had been delivered by the jury who stated Evelyn Foster was the victim of: 'Murder by person or person's unknown.' To all intents and purpose the Foster case was finally closed. The following day the police presence was severely scaled down as the police vacated Otterburn Tower and the police officers returned to their various stations. All documentation on the Foster case was parcelled up and sent to divisional HQ at Hexham. The public hearing may well have ended however, the trial by press had not. The so called statement by Fullarton James had been released by the *Daily Express*. The local press, probably feeling more than a little piqued at having been beaten to a scoop by a national newspaper, wanted to know if the Chief Constable had, in fact, issued this statement so that they could at least publish their version. Fullarton James was not to be forced into making any further statements and refused to discuss the matter. His refusal, however, gave more credence to the fact that he may have issued the statement. As has been seen throughout the Foster case, when doubts rear their head they are hard to dispel and to this end, Fullarton James allowed a statement to be released to the press by Superintendent Taylor on his behalf: 'The Chief Constable does not feel himself free to make any statement in regard to the matter.' Short, sweet and to the point.

The full statement, considering it had been given before the verdict was passed, is damning against the Chief Constable as it is not only his personal thoughts that are aired but, a statement on behalf of the Northumberland County Constabulary: 'I know how strong the local feeling is. We must accept the murder verdict, because there is no appeal against it.

At the same time I am convinced that a verdict of murder is against the weight of the evidence. We have made enquiries not only in Northumberland but in Scotland and almost every County in England.

We are satisfied that the motor car in which Miss Foster's supposed murderer is said to have travelled from Jedburgh does not exist. We are also satisfied that the man she described does not exist.

I believe the girl set fire to the motor car herself, but it is impossible to say definitely why she should do so. I have never believed that the motive was an insurance fraud. I think it more likely, as the coroner suggested, that she was a hysterical girl who was obsessed with a desire for publicity or that she was suffering from an abnormality.' If this statement had been issued by Fullarton James then it was clearly wrong of him to do so. The first three paragraphs are fair enough as he is the policeman in charge of the investigation. The fourth paragraph is highly subjective and he really had no experience to pass this as a judgement. It is clear to see why such a statement upset the Foster family in particular Joseph.

Joseph Foster was to have his day however. On 24 March 1931, an inquiry was to be held in the Moot Hall, Newcastle. Of his so-called statement in the *Daily Express*, Fullarton James was to state: 'With regard to the paragraph in Mr J.J. Foster's letter to the Secretary of State alleging that I made a statement on the verdict of the coroner's jury to a newspaper reporter, I wish to say that no such statement was made. I did, however, have what I considered a confidential conversation with a reporter about two hours before the jury returned their verdict. I had no idea the conversation would be published, and

I complained to the editor of the newspaper in question immediately I saw a paragraph in it which purported to set out a summary of the conversation.'

It may be seen that Fullarton James was as much a victim in that what he stated was supposed to be off the record and not for publication. A scenario much more associated with modern-day journalism. However, off the record or not, he should not have stated what he put forward in paragraph three: this was purely subjective. As a Chief Constable, he should have shown a bit more sense than offer-up statements to the press in the hope that they would not be published. Much space was given to the fact that Joseph Foster, and a committee of friends, sought evidence to 'confirm' the jury's verdict. No doubt they continued to look for more evidence into what had happened on the night of 6 January 1931 that is quite understandable. However, the jury's verdict of 'Murder by person or person's unknown' did not need to be confirmed; the jury and the coroner had already confirmed it. The police did make it clear that they remained open to any further evidence, if any were to turn up however, none appeared to do so. The official verdict stands and that is the way it will remain.

Notes.

1) Goodman: Makes a statement that: Joseph Foster grabbed constable Fergusson's arm. There is no real evidence to support this and it may well be nothing more than village gossip, passed on by word of mouth and now taken as fact.

2) Goodman, p 41

3) Goodman, P 46.

4) Goodman makes a point in noting the doors of the Hudson were in various stages of openness. Most press photographs were taken during Wednesday and, presumably after 3-30 pm When Inspector Russell arrived on the scene. The car was guarded prior to this.

5) Julian Symons. '*A Reasonable Doubt*', The Cresset Press 1960. Chapter '*The Invisible Man,* P 190. Symons claims a journalist told him: An enterprising Journalist went out to Wolf's Nick, examined the car and placed Evelyn's scarf over a headlamp and possibly left the footprint from which the police took a mould. This was second-hand and thirty years after the event: it could be bragging on the part of the modern-day journalist or plain stupidity on the part of the original reporter. Either way it can only be seen as foolishness.

6) Both Symons and Goodman refer to the lack of CID during the Foster case.

7) Dodds John. F. '*Bastions And Belligerents: Medieval Strongholds In Northumberland*' Keepdate Publishing Ltd. 1999. P 334.

8) Goodman refers to Mrs X, P 132 – 135.

CHAPTER FOUR

THE JOURNEY TO NOWHERE.

The general outline of the story, as we have it from Evelyn Foster, is fairly well known however, one part of it has always remained open to question and has in reality never been fully answered. The question is, where did Evelyn go on her final drive? The police attempted to form a theory that Evelyn drove her car no further than the point known as Wolf's Nick. On the other hand, the Foster family and their supporters held fast to the theory that Evelyn drove her car as far as the village of Belsay. The story originated from Evelyn as she told it to her mother. It was under questioning from her mother that Evelyn revealed that she travelled not only to Belsay but, the far side of Belsay; in this she was emphatic, her mother asking her twice. After reaching a point beyond Belsay, under instruction from the *strange man* who was supposedly with her, she turned the car north again towards Otterburn. For one reason or another, either she, or the *strange man*, stopped the car on the road at a point called Wolf's Nick; the sole purpose for doing this appears to be the destruction of her car by fire on the moors at Wolf's Nick.

Evelyn's journey began shortly after 6-30 pm. The Foster bus from Hexham pulled up in the forecourt of the Percy Arms and deposited most of its passengers as well as the conductor, Tommy Rutherford, who was to deliver parcels from Hexham. One of these parcels was sausages for Otterburn teacher, Mary Ferry. The bus then proceeded up the street and parked in the garage forecourt. Of the remaining passengers, most dispersed into their houses in the west end of Otterburn; three were to remain. Of these three, two were men going on to Rochester and one was a woman, Mary Murray, going on to Cottonshopeburn Foot.

These three passengers, as part of the Foster service, would be taken further on up the valley in Evelyn's taxi. Gordon Foster, after checking the number of passengers 'going on' with driver Cecil Johnstone, crossed the road to the Kennels in order to give the numbers to Evelyn Foster. Evelyn, dressed in her uniform of heavy tweed coat, brown, woollen scarf and brown felt hat then crossed from the Kennels and ushered her passengers into the waiting Hudson. The journey from Otterburn to Cottonshopeburn Foot was, according to police measurements, just over eight miles. Some of the road was very twisty for most of the way and, in particular, the area around Elishaw Road Ends and towards Horsley, a small hamlet just short of Rochester.

With the two men dropped off at Rochester, Evelyn and Mrs Mary Murray began to exchange local gossip. Mary Murray was well known to Evelyn and also a regular customer, this was carried on for a while as they sat at the roadside before Mary Murray departed the taxi to walk up the track to her home. As Mary Murray got out of the taxi, a car passed travelling towards Otterburn: all that Mary Murray could say about it was it was a big car with high top and bright lights. Evelyn then turned her Hudson in the gateway of Birdhopecraig Farm, a convenient point to turn her car due to the narrowness of the road, and began the drive back to Otterburn. As she approached Elishaw Road Ends a car was sitting in the junction to Dere Street and it was from this car that a man approached and flagged Evelyn's taxi down.

The waiting car would suggest that someone in the car had prior knowledge of Evelyn's taxi travelling on the road at this time; not difficult for anyone living in the area of Otterburn, and knew that it was travelling to Otterburn. However, the distance of just over two miles to Otterburn would have been little hardship to anyone travelling to Hexham, a mere diversion, such as in the story given by Evelyn to her mother. It has been suggested that this car belonged to a woman who lived along Dere Street at its most southern end.[1] If this were true then the detour would once again be slight almost to the point of making no difference. Once again, if this were true, the mystery woman knowing Evelyn's car then, likewise, Evelyn would surely have known the woman's car and, it can be suggested, would have also known the woman driver. So sparse was the traffic in Otterburn in 1931 that everyone knew everyone else's car: even more so if the car owner was a woman. Evelyn was later to say that a woman occupied the driver's seat of the car, this she could see well as her car stood in the headlights of the Hudson. Considering the nature of the twisty road and the frosty conditions, Evelyn completed the round journey in less than thirty minutes and would give her an average speed of around twenty-three miles an hour.

A statement by Albert Beach,[2] a travelling steam-roller driver, appeared to back up Evelyn's statement at this point. On 6 January, Albert Beach had been working in the vicinity of Elishaw and had his caravan parked at Elishaw Bridge, around a quarter of a mile down Dere Street from the road end. He left his caravan at around 6-45 pm, to travel into Otterburn with his friend, John Oliver, for a drink at the pub, he was immediately passed by a car travelling, or, as he put it, 'tearing down' Dere Street from the main road. The speed of the car so impressed Albert Beach that he commented on the fact to his friend, however, travelling fast or not, Albert Beach was able to describe the car: 'I am absolutely certain that this car was a two-seater, covered in, and it seemed dark blue.' Albert Beach further added: 'I thought the first car (on Dere Street) was a Morris Cowley two seater but I am not certain.' Robert Townes, a gardener, also noted the fast moving car on Dere Street as it passed Albert Beach; Robert Townes was only a short distance further down the road.

Albert Beach then took a short cut across a field to gain the Otterburn to Jedburgh road. It was while crossing this field that he stated: 'I saw a motor car going towards Otterburn on the main road.' This was some five minutes later and about two-hundred yards from Elishaw Bridge. This appears to have been a busy time in Otterburn even if no one else seemed to notice. As Albert Beach walked along the main road, just passed Otterburn School, he was passed by a motor bike; no one else appears to have seen this. It was travelling from the north, towards Otterburn and: 'It was going very slow due to the road conditions.' Albert Beach noted also, that he passed a man at this time who was walking north. This man appeared to be a workman as:' He had a 'bait bag' over his shoulder and was wearing an overcoat. The man he described as: 'A short, thick-set man who appeared to have been working with lime, it was on his boots, he did not speak.' Presumably, Albert Beach was still in the dark at this time as he had not reached Otterburn; this he did at 7-30 pm as he noticed the Foster bus arrive from Newcastle with the papers.

Evelyn's Hudson was next witnessed by George Maughan and his wife as they left their house, next to the Co-Op building where George Maughan worked, and were on their way to Otterburn School where George Maughan looked after the fires. The Co-Op building was a mere hundred yards down the street from the Kennels. George Maughan was to state that they left around 7-pm give or take a minute either way as soon as they left they noticed a cars headlights approaching from the direction of Rochester. George Maughan was to emphasise that he had the car in view until it came to a halt outside the Kennels; this coincided with his arrival at the same spot. He was within four or five feet of the offside of the Hudson: 'I knew this was Foster's car and I saw a woman driving it. I did not see anyone beside her or anyone in the car. I am not prepared to say that anyone was sitting in the front – but there may have been. I did not see anyone get out.'

At this time Robert Luke, a bus driver for the Foster's, was due to finish his shift. He walked outside the garage, noting the time, as the garage clock struck seven and crossed the road to the Kennels to get some wire he needed. As he crossed the road he noticed the Hudson sitting at the petrol pumps and, at the same time saw George Maughan and his wife pass the car. Without stopping he passed a remark to George Maughan: 'I remarked to Maughan something about secretly courting his wife again and his wife said something in reply and they walked on without stopping.' Although he passed close to the car Robert Luke noted: 'I then for the first time saw the Hudson car standing at the petrol pump, just inside the wicket in front of Mr Foster's house.' Robert Luke saw no one, apart from George Maughan and his wife, around the car; there was no movement between the Kennels and the petrol pump at this time.

One other man was supposedly passing the Foster garage at this time: this was John Thompson. The statement of John Thompson is fraught with problems and only leaves the reader full of doubts. His original statement begins with a timing of 7 pm and, after a paragraph, is subsequently crossed out before it begins again with the entry of 7-15 pm. John Thompson was a farm labourer at Garretshiels Farm, a farm about a mile to the west of Otterburn but nearer the Elishaw road. After finishing work, John Thompson normally walked home to Otterburn. He walked across a field and crossed the River Rede by a small footbridge from where he gained the Otterburn road shortly after it passed Otterburn School: it was at this point that his statement began.

As he was walking the road, just south of the school, John Thompson was passed by a car, at 7-15 pm, travelling in the direction of Otterburn. Unfortunately, unlike George Maughan, he failed to say if, or for how long he kept this car in sight. However, he passed a car standing outside the Kennels, on his reckoning of time this would have been about 7-23 pm. About some ten yards south of Foster's garage, he states, he met two men: '...whom I could not recognise.' He could not say what they were like but only observed that one of these men: '...had leggings on'.

Goodman has him identifying a man with leggings on standing at the petrol pumps when, according to Goodman, Evelyn was filling her car with petrol.[3] This would appear to be a misinterpretation by Goodman rather than a mistake by John Thompson as Thompson did state that he recognised a woman's voice, at the petrol pumps, as that of Evelyn Foster. The statement by Goodman, pointed to the fact that the woman could have been Dorothy, Evelyn's sister, as she was in the habit of wearing long woollen socks that could be mistaken, especially in the dark, for leggings.

On his own admission, John Thompson, was only about one-hundred yards south of Otterburn School at 7-15 pm. At this time, Evelyn had already departed Otterburn. To walk into Otterburn would take about a further eight minutes, taking his time up to around 7-23 pm; at this time, Evelyn was reliably reported as having been seen at Raylees Farm, some two miles east of Otterburn. However, John Thompson, saw a car standing at the petrol pumps when he arrived in Otterburn. John Thompson's timings, it should be pointed out, were not based on checking the time with a watch but, based on his past experience of walking home each night: they were, therefore, not truly accurate timings, only what he thought they should be.

Like George Maughan's statement, there is an inclusion at the bottom of John Thompson's statement, again added in ink. The words of this inclusion read; 'I am sure the man I saw was Maughan, at the time.' Given the discrepancies in the timing alone, as well as some of the evidence, why was it felt necessary to have the inclusion? Did John Thompson have a sudden flash of afterthought or jolt of his memory? Or was it a simple fact that the change was at the suggestion of the Police, bringing two unidentified men, the one seen by John Thompson and the one noted by George Maughan at the Church gate, and placing them together therefore removing any trace of an unidentified man in Otterburn Village at that time? For whatever reason, the Coroner failed to question it and, in retrospect, they should have been challenged on the timing alone.

On her arrival back at the 'Kennels' Evelyn had given a brief resume of her encounter with the man at Elishaw to her mother. The first words to her mother being: 'I've brought a man down from Elishaw. He wants to go to Ponteland to catch the bus.' While Evelyn was topping up the car with petrol, her mother was relating the story to Evelyn's father while asking him for an estimate of the fare. Evelyn's younger sister, Dorothy, on overhearing the story, suggested that Evelyn take her friend George Philipson, an employee of the Foster's as well as a friend of Evelyn's, living in the bothy a short distance down the street from the 'Kennels', to accompany her as a chaperon companion. Her mother agreed with this, telling Evelyn: 'Take him, call and get him as you go through the village.' This Evelyn agreed to with the words: 'All right mother' as she picked up a flashlight her final words as she departed were: 'I'll take your flashlight mother'. She then departed the house for her moorland destiny.

However, there is no evidence at all that Evelyn called at the bothy and neither did she see, or ask, George Philipson to accompany her.

Nothing more was thought of the matter until Evelyn's youngest sister, Margaret, arrived home from her work as a conductress on a bus an hour or so later and casually stated that she had seen George Philipson on the street. The modern-day cynic would suggest there were only two reasons for this: Evelyn knew the man and did not want George Philipson to be there or, plain and simple, there was no man at all. Local knowledge from that period would rubbish the former as utter nonsense however; neither would they be too keen on the second suggestion.

In some of the writing's on the Evelyn Foster case as well as some of the witness statements, there is some confusion as to where Evelyn's car stood: outside the 'Kennels' or the garage? The garage stands on the north side of the street while the 'Kennels' stands on the south side almost directly opposite. At the time of the events, the petrol pumps stood outside the 'Kennels', to the left of the wicket gate as you look at the house. The garage was used for the maintenance side of the business. When Evelyn needed to fill her taxi's petrol tank, she did so outside the 'Kennels' therefore; anyone in the garage across the road could not see Evelyn's taxi unless they came out of the garage as Robert Luke did that night. The petrol pumps were divided from the garden by a small wall with a wicket gate. In later years the petrol pumps and the storage tank were removed from outside the 'Kennels'. A local man remembers this happening and it was he who was to rebuild the stone wall at the front of the house, a wall that still stands.

According to Evelyn's evidence, she was now to meet the man at the 'Percy Arms' Hotel, at the east end of Otterburn. The man was going there to find a lift or, if not successful, then await Evelyn either outside the hotel or on the end of the bridge that spans the Otter Burn to the east of the Percy Arms. Likewise, Evelyn would visit the 'Percy Arms' looking for this man. The 'Percy Arms' was not the size that it is today neither did it have the staff of the present-day hotel nor the clientele, especially on a cold, winters night. Only two staff was on duty that night: Gladys Tatham, in the lounge and John Scott in the public bar. Gladys Tatham was not only a worker; she was also the daughter of the landlord of the Percy Arms. As far as her duties went that night, she was in charge of the lounge and had been all that day, from 8am to 10-30pm. She acknowledged that:

'I know Evelyn Foster very well and can say definitely that she never called at the hotel between 6pm and 10-30pm.' Evelyn used to visit the 'Percy Arms' on a regular basis in connection with her taxi business. She would visit the 'Percy Arms' to enquire after any messages left for her or any enquiries about her business. On these occasions, Gladys Tatham was to say, Evelyn would use the front door.

John Scott was the second member of staff who was on duty at the 'Percy Arms' that night. John Scott's employment at the 'Percy Arms' was twofold: not only was he barman, he was also the chauffeur of the hotels hire car. In both capacities John Scott was in a good position to note the coming and going of anyone, stranger or not, into the pub. John Scott was on duty in the public bar between the hours of 6-20 pm and 8-20 pm. He also knew Evelyn Foster very well due to her comings and goings on taxi business as well as knowing her through their mutual business of car hire. John Scott was to state: 'I can say definitely that she never called between these hours, his on duty hours, to enquire if any man had left word to say they had got a lift to Ponteland.' He was also to point out that there was no strange man 'with a brown hat' while he was on duty. The public bar would have been the natural place to enter in order to enquire about a lift to Ponteland or anywhere else. If a strange man, or anyone else, was to enquire about a lift to anywhere, then surely anyone within the vicinity of the 'Percy Arms' would have directed them to John Scott. That no one did surely must lend strength to the argument that there was no man in the first place.

It would appear that there were quite a few people on the street that night between 7 pm and 7-30 pm. Some saw others while some were to note that they saw a strange man on the street as well. However, none were to note seeing a car during this period. If Evelyn's story is to be believed, she drove her taxi down the street to the bothy in order to pick up George Philipson, a distance of only a hundred yards. Presumably, after stopping the car, she went in leaving her car headlights on yet, no one saw her do it or even saw a car and, in those days, there was no street lighting in Otterburn: the only lighting was from the widows of the buildings and that would not be much. She would then drive down the street to the bridge, a mere few yards further, opposite the 'Percy Arms'. From witnesses statements we know that she did not enter the 'Percy Arms' which leaves us to believe that she picked up the man from on or near the bridge. There were two witnesses in the vicinity of the bridge, both teachers, both observant yet neither reported seeing the car but both saw a man.

After leaving the 'Kennels' at around 7-10 pm, there is no reliable sighting of Evelyn Foster until she was found at Wolf's Nick. Her car was reliably identified when it passed Raylees Farm at 7-22 pm. Evelyn's Hudson appears to have proceeded down the main Otterburn street, a total of 293 yards, from the 'Kennels' to the bridge over the Otter Burn, without once being identified or even noticed. However, there were people on the Otterburn main street at this time. George Maughan had witnessed a strange man as had John Thompson; the timing of John Thompson is suspect however. Yet, the addition to George Maughan's statement clearly states that the man he saw was John Thompson. This addition was written in ink at the bottom of a typewritten statement and merely states: 'I saw John Thompson'. This addition along with the addition to John Thompson's statement will be discussed later.

It is possible, of course, that both Maughan and Thompson saw the same man whom neither recognised. The statement of George Maughan was proved reliable. At this time, however, he was off the street having passed Evelyn's Hudson at the Kennels. George Sinclair was also on the same part of the street as Maughan and Thompson. His timing though fits with Thompsons rather than Maughans. He was also to see a strange man outside the Post Office. The difference here is that the strange man was on the same side of the street as Maughan. Once again, it could have been the same strange man, as witnessed by Maughan but now having crossed the street. Could this also have been the same strange man who was seen by Miss Annie Carruthers and Miss Annie Ferry in the vicinity of the bridge? Oddly, none of these nocturnal travellers noticed Evelyn's Hudson as it passed down the street.

George Philipson was to make a statement to *The Evening World*. After first pointing out how distressed he was he moved on to the events of the night of 6 January. He had arrived at the Foster garage and made enquiries about Evelyn only to be told that she had just departed. No one at the garage knew that Evelyn was going on any lengthy journey, she could have been going only to the other end of the street however, George Philipson took it as going on a journey without the village, and he was to state: 'If one of her sisters had been well – she would have accompanied Evelyn on the ride.' For some reason, George Philipson left the garage in a seemingly anxious state, why he was so anxious is not made clear. On leaving the garage he said that he saw Evelyn's Hudson disappearing out of the village. This would be just a few yards east of the bridge as trees blocked any further view. His statement does beg one question; if George Philipson arrived at the garage as he said then he must have been on the street at the same time as Evelyn's Hudson passed down it. He had only seen the rear lights, had the car been standing still and in the process of moving off? The distance from the garage to the 'Percy Arms' is less than three-hundred yards; due to a bend at this point as well as trees, this is as far as anyone can see. George Philipson's statement also begs the question: could he have been the *strange man* seen by George Sinclair and possibly Mary ferry? He was noted as in an anxious state.

After leaving Otterburn, the road passes the Elsdon junction and steadily begins its climb out of the Rede Valley. Some two miles further on the road bends to the left and climbs up from a dip before cresting a rise just before Raylees Farm. Important to remember at this point is the fact that the roads were hazardous with a heavy winter frost. The road from this point, until it reaches Wolf's Nick is a series of turns, bends and sharp corners while at the same time climbing steeply out of the Rede Valley. The Hudson Super Six, driven by Evelyn, had a sixty horse power engine driving wheels with a six inch tread width through a three speed gearbox, the car itself, was somewhat top heavy, compared to modern day cars, and would be a bit cumbersome to drive, especially in conditions of heavy frost. I have driven a more modern car over this route in the frost of November and, although a lot more flexible, engine wise and technically better at road holding, it could not be driven above thirty miles an hour before the wheels began spinning on the slippery surface.

John Robson was the driver of the Foster bus on the route from Newcastle to Otterburn. He had left Newcastle at around five or ten minutes past six after having been delayed awaiting the arrival of an incoming bus. At 6-40 pm the bus had arrived in Belsay, John Robson knew this for certain after checking the time on the clock at the saddlers shop. His next scheduled stop was to be at Raylees Farm. The farm sits back slightly from the road and the bus conductor, having jumped down from the bus, crossed the road in order to leave the newspapers on the garden wall. Sitting in his cab, John Robson then noticed the approaching headlights of a car and dipped the headlights of the bus.

John Robson was to state: 'When the car got up to me I recognised it as Mr Foster's Hudson. I looked at my watch and noticed it was 7-22 pm. The Hudson would not be doing more than ten miles an hour and going in the direction of Newcastle.' Even at that relatively slow speed, John Robson was unable to say who was driving the Hudson as he had been temporarily blinded by the oncoming headlights. Some have queried why the Hudson should be going so slowly on a main road. Evelyn Foster would have known that this was the Foster bus and would be delivering the papers to Raylees Farm. It would be quite natural for her to slow down as she approached the bus as the conductor would not have been easy to see as he crossed the road.

Raylees Farm was the last reliable sighting of Evelyn Foster's Hudson. The next statement for the Police must be ranked as one of the oddest statements to be put before the Coroner. This was the statement of Robert Edwin Harrison. Robert Harrison was also a bus driver, employed by Robert Tait and Son. The Tait bus company, although running a local bus service, was not in direct competition with the Foster busses. The Tait busses served mainly to the east side of the Newcastle to Otterburn road between Knowesgate and Morpeth although some routes took them in the direction of Ponteland. Robert Harrison lived at Longwitton Station, some five miles east of Knowesgate. Harrison was to state that he left Knowesgate at 7-30 pm. Like other bus drivers, we can take his timing as reasonably accurate as he was used to running to a timetable. However, at this point his statement has already ruled itself out as useless. Evelyn Foster's Hudson had been reliably noted as at Raylees Farm at 7-22 pm. Although in his statement, Robert Harrison was to state that, Knowesgate was four miles south of Raylees Farm in actual fact it is almost six miles south.

Continuing at a speed of around twenty miles an hour average, Evelyn Foster could not have arrived at Knowesgate before 7-40 pm: some ten minutes after Harrison had left. It would appear that the Police had entered this witness's statement to support their theory that Evelyn Foster had never travelled beyond Wolfs Nick. At the time Harrison left Knowesgate, Evelyn Foster's Hudson was still climbing out of the Rede Valley, south of Raylees Farm. To further muddy the waters, Harrison was to state: '...close to Ferney Chesters I met a car travelling north. I can't describe the car; I knew her old car but not her new car.' Ferney Chesters is some four miles south of Knowesgate. It is possible that the Police would have thought it strengthened their case somewhat if Harrison had seen the car coming from Newcastle. This would have strengthened the possibility that Evelyn Foster had never got as far as Belsay. As it was, the Coroner did not query the times of Harrisons statement.

From the point of leaving Raylees Farm, we only have Evelyn Foster's account of what was to happen next. Even this was only second-hand as it was passed on by her mother. The road from Raylees Farm rises slightly for a short distance before it takes a sharp right at Ravenscleugh Farm. From here the road rises quickly and steeply as well as negotiating a number of twists and turns of varying severity. The average speed of the Hudson at this time could have been only around twenty miles an hour at the most, and probably far less, due to not only the nature of the road but, also the condition of the surface due to heavy frost. The road remains like this as it passes Ottercops Farm until it reaches its highest point, the cleft in the rock formation known as Wolf's Nick, some eight miles south of Otterburn. After this point the road ceases to climb and also straightens out. Although the nature of the road becomes more traffic friendly, it is still in the wide open countryside and susceptible to frost. Evelyn could, in reality, have picked up a little more speed over this stretch.

During this period, according to Evelyn, the man, spoke a lot about cars and seemed knowledgeable on the subject as well as smoking a lot. They then passed through Belsay, she was emphatic about this, her mother queried it with a; 'Are you sure'? 'Yes mother, because I met two cars coming from Newcastle which I thought I knew. One was Mr Kirsopp-Reed's, the other I was not sure of.' William

Kirsopp-Reed was a local Otterburn farmer; his farm was Old Town Farm on the Otterburn to Dere Street road, had been on the road that night. He had travelled from Newcastle where he had been with some other family members. He was to state: 'I proceeded by Belsay. When about two-hundred yards north of the lodge at the north end of Belsay, I met a motor car proceeding south. It would be between 7-15 and 7-20 pm'. At this time, Evelyn was leaving Raylees Farm so this car could certainly not have been hers. William Kirsopp-Reed goes on to state that he passed a stationary car at Bradford Bank but, this was still south of Ferney Chesters and the crunch of his statement, as far as Evelyn Foster is concerned, came with, at Harle (Kirkharle) almost two miles south of Knowesgate, 'I passed a Tait's bus'. This could only be Robert Harrison's bus. And, as we have seen, Evelyn's Hudson was some way behind this bus. William Kirsopp-Reed was to further state that: 'I do not remember passing any other cars'. An addition, in ink, at the bottom clearly states: 'I know Miss Foster's car. I did not see it.'

An odd statement for Evelyn to make was that she had passed two cars near Belsay, one she recognised as the car of Kirsopp-Reed. If the timing of Kirsopp-Reed is correct then he left a point north of Belsay at between 7-15 pm and 7-20 pm, a time when Evelyn was known to have been approaching Raylees Farm some fifteen miles to the north. At a speed of around twenty miles an hour, Evelyn could not possibly have been at that point until around 8-05 PM. Allowing for each car to be travelling at an average of twenty miles an hour coupled with a little conjecture, the two cars should have passed somewhere in the region of Capheaton at around 7-50 pm. Given a little leeway, in both directions, could these have been the cars, two travelling south and one north, that had passed John Kennedy as he walked from Kirkwhelpington to Knowesgate at *around* 8 pm? The distance from where John Kennedy saw the cars to where the cars were estimated to pass each other, is a mere two miles.

A point also to bear in mind is that, Kirsopp-Reed passed Tait's bus at Kirkharle and Evelyn's taxi was some way behind Tait's bus. However, after passing Tait's bus, Kirsopp-Reed, could not remember passing any other vehicles. Evelyn had stated clearly that she had passed two cars near Belsay, one was: 'Mr Kirsopp-Reed's'. If Evelyn had not seen this car how could she have possibly known that it was even on the road that night? In the coroner's court, Kirsopp-Reed was to admit that he had told Evelyn's brother, Gordon that he was going to Newcastle that day. The question remains; how did Evelyn know the exact timing of Kirsopp-Reed's car so that she could say that they passed at an exact spot?

It was around this time that the amicable man appeared to change into some kind of beast. As the Hudson passed through Belsay, some eleven miles south of Knowesgate, the man no longer wanted to carry on to Ponteland: in fact he wanted to return to Otterburn. He now also appears to be sick of Evelyn's driving as he stated that he wanted to drive. According to Evelyn's statement, given by her mother 'She felt him creep along the seat towards her'. On protesting, Evelyn received a punch above the eye while the man grabbed the steering wheel of the car. This presumably left Evelyn working the pedals of the car, neither she nor anyone else gave mention to this.

Whether working the pedals or just the steering wheel, this would have been an odd and very difficult manoeuvre to carry out. It would be possible, although awkward, to steer the car from this position, the left side of the wheel would be almost central in the car. However, for someone on the passenger side to work the pedals would be extremely difficult, even more so if the 'driver' had put up any kind of resistance at all. One point to remember is that anyone sitting in the driver's seat would have made it difficult for the car to be driven like this. Evelyn, although not fat by any means was a little on the 'dumpy' side. Add to this the fact that she was wearing heavy winter clothing and it can be seen that there was little room for anyone to manoeuvre in the front seat. However, Evelyn would have us believe that the man drove the car in this position for some eleven miles, on a frost and ice covered road, back to Wolf's Nick.

John Kennedy, a road-mender by profession was walking home to Knowesgate after an early evening out at Kirkwhelpington. He had left Kirkwhelpington at around 8 pm and set off northwards. At around 8-10 pm he was passed by a saloon car travelling northwards, towards Otterburn; 'At high speed'. Most car drivers questioned have given their average speed no higher than thirty miles an hour down to as low as thirteen miles an hour. There is no exact speed given for this car, however, 'high speed' is taken as somewhere in the region of over thirty miles an hour and, due to the road conditions, even this appears a little high. The road at this point, although reasonably straight, with the odd few bends, is fairly narrow and not much more than what would be classed today as a country lane. John Kennedy goes on to state with confidence: 'I noticed that a man was driving, but saw no one else in the car; I am unable to say whether the driver wore a bowler hat or any head covering'. This statement was made some ten days after the night of 6 January and is more than a little suspect.

Once again a statement begs the question; how can anyone tell what a driver looks like in the dark? Only the head and shoulders show at the best of times. The latter part, concerning a bowler hat, only became common knowledge after a day or so after the police had issued a description. It is doubtful therefore, if a bowler hat would register or, even be noticeable, in a car travelling at 'high speed'. John Kennedy was to state, more than once, that he only saw the face of the man. He still maintained these views, described by the coroner as 'remarkable', after the enquiry: at least he was consistent if nothing else.

Some questions do appear to spring to mind. If this man was the stranger that Evelyn would have us believe he was why, when they arrived at Belsay, within less than five miles of relative civilisation, would he want to return to Otterburn, a place he had little or no knowledge of? If he intended to harm or even kill Evelyn, how would he make his escape across wild moorland on a winter's night?

As the car passed through Belsay, a small village, and presumably Evelyn was working the pedals of the car, why did she not apply the brakes? Evelyn must have had some control of the pedals. Even the handbrake on the Hudson was on the right hand side of the car, between Evelyn and the door. To have hit a wall or something similar would surely have brought some kind of immediate rescue. If Evelyn had applied any kind of resistance at all, the man would certainly have had difficulty keeping the car on the road. On this lonely stretch of moorland road how could any stranger to the area have singled a place out like Wolf's Nick in order to run a car off the road? They would have passed it going south however; a stranger to the area would hardly register the fact.

There is also the question, why did the man drive the car so far before he set fire to it? In effect, according to Evelyn's story, he chose to drive a car for some eleven miles in a most uncomfortable position and, in all this time, he was not fully in control of the car that was travelling on a sometimes twisting and frost covered road; a road that was also unfamiliar to him. It has also been written: 'There was practically no other spot along this road where a car could have been driven on to the moor.' [4] From Belsay to Knowesgate the road is bordered by open fields: it can be said that a car in a field would draw attention. However, from Wolf's Nick, for some seven miles in a northerly direction, the road is completely bordered by wild, open moorland.

THE BURNT HUDSON ON THE MOOR

Along any part of that road, much of it unfenced in 1931, to just short of Otterburn, a car could safely be driven off the road and set on fire.

The next stop on the journey was: 'The top of the hill of Wolf's Nick.' Based on the average speed of the car being around twenty miles an hour, the whole of the journey, from Otterburn to Belsay then the return to Wolf's Nick would have taken around one and a half hours and covered some twenty-nine miles. All that was left to do was to drive the car across the road and over the shoulder on the far side. On this final part of the journey, the car crossed the road at an angle of some forty-five degrees. In this way the car hit the verge at a right angle, very near straight on, had it not then the car would most certainly have rolled over. It has been suggested that the car was driven down the embankment. This must surely be a bit fanciful. The embankment at this point drops some four to five feet at a steep angle. If the car had crossed the shoulder of the road even a yard or so further along than it did, it would have been faced with an even steeper drop. According to one writer: 'To drive the car down the bank was a tricky and even dangerous operation'.[5] Tricky and dangerous it certainly was as this was a drop rather than just a 'run down' the bank.

For exactly how long the car had been parked at its roadside halt of Wolf's Nick, it is impossible to say. It is important to note that, the name Wolf's Nick, in reality, means the area of. The point where the car entered the moor is some one-hundred and twenty yards further on. However, the car was there long enough, according to Evelyn's statement, for the man to carry out some kind of fiendish assault, before the car was driven over the embankment. The word 'driven' is used in most reports and statements and is mostly thought of as the car was under some sort of control: there is no real evidence of anyone being in the driver's seat at this time. The word 'driven' is loosely applied to describe that the car was under some kind of power or control.

William Jennings, a motor engineer from Morpeth who was later to inspect the car, was to state: 'The car was in low gear and the engine on idle and with the handbrake in the off position'. The Hudson, like many cars of the period, was fitted with a hand throttle control that allowed the engine to 'tick-over' at a higher RPM. With the hand throttle set at idle, the car, on a reasonably flat surface, could travel under its own volition for an indefinite period. The only other way of stopping it was if it was stopped by either switching off the control or the car meeting with an object that it could not surmount, hence stalling the engine.

The Hudson mounted the embankment offside, driver's side, and offside front wheel first, it was that side that first dropped over the embankment. This, William Jennings was to prove by the scrapes on the bottom of the car's running board left by the stones embedded in the bank.[6] The car then dropped, rather than being driven, down the bank for some four to five feet. As the car hit the surface of the moor, its front wheel tracks were erratic causing William Jennings to comment that the car was out of control. At this point, due to the lie of the land, the moor drops away to the left before climbing slightly if viewed straight on from the car; this caused the car to turn slightly to its left as it crossed the moor. The speed during its journey across the moor at this time was estimated at around no more than ten miles an hour; this was calculated by Jennings from the settings of the car as well as the lie of the land. Due to the surface of the moor rising, the Hudson was in a constant left turn, its wheels leaving tracks some eight to ten inches deep in places, in the boggy surface, until it met one of the numerous draining ditches on the moor. At this point it was turned even further left until its wheels, in a slight uphill direction, met a small dry ditch which caused the engine to finally stall and the Hudson came to a halt facing the road from where it had come: its journey finally over, its wheels still on left lock.

NOTES.

1) Jonathan Goodman   'The Burning Of Evelyn Foster'   David and Charles 1977. Page 132.

2) Police Statement, Coroners Report, (Albert Beach) Northumberland Archives COS/3/54/1.

3) Goodman   P 90.

4) Julian Symons   '*A Reasonable Doubt*'   The Cresset Press 1960. P 193.

5) Ibid   P 193.

6) Police Statement, Coroners Report, (William Jennings) Northumberland Archives COS/3/54/1.

CHAPTER FIVE.

THE INVISIBLE MAN AND THE MYSTERY WOMAN.

Anyone who likes a good thriller, whether it's in written form, drama or film, knows that the essential part is the part is that which dwells on the unseen, the mystery or invisible person. He or she appears from nowhere and saves the main figure of the plot or, alternatively, carries out the dastardly deed. After the deed is done, good or bad, they retreat into the mists or the wild moorland never to be seen again. It all adds to the tension of the story and gives the medium a feeling of 'what if'? The invisible or mystery person gives a whole new dimension to the story; gives it a punch-line and leaves the reader or viewer with a memory that troubles the sleep. Perhaps the mystery person will enter that most sacred realm of our personality, the land of dreams as well. The invisible person has the ability to gain entry into the farthest corners of our mind and eat away at our mind; it can do anything: nowhere is safe. On the other hand, it can give that extra kick to any story that little bit of something that is lacking. The invisible person has the ability to turn a mediocre story into a memorable or everlasting one. Without doubt it is the invisible person that has turned the Evelyn Foster case into something different, this is not a straightforward murder story, it is a memorable one. Without the invisible person as an ingredient, the Evelyn Foster case would have slipped into history as just another murder case.

In the case of Evelyn Foster, one invisible person is just not enough. We have two and this has given the case an even deeper perspective. On one hand we have a man, an *invisible* man who is looking for a bus to take him to Newcastle, in the middle of the Northumberland moors on a cold, winter's night. To add to the depth of the story, he was delivered there by a car driven by – who knows? We have only the story to turn to for evidence and that leads us only to – a mystery woman. Who, we have now to ask, gave us the mystery woman? And the answer would be, the *invisible* man. On the surface, it is Evelyn Foster who gave us both the *invisible* man and the mystery woman. At about 7 pm on the night of 6 January, Evelyn Foster entered the Foster house and uttered the immortal words: 'I have brought a man down from Elishaw and he wants to go to Ponteland to catch a bus.'[1] This man had alighted from a car in the vicinity of Elishaw Road Ends. Although the car was seen by Evelyn, in the full glare of her car's headlights; all she could say about it was: 'The car was dark coloured and closed.' Evelyn's mother was later to add: 'She said there was a woman in the driver's seat of the car.' The mystery woman was now born.

Evidence given by Albert Beach, a steam – roller driver, appeared, at least on the surface, to corroborate the evidence given by Evelyn Foster. As stated previous, he saw a car: 'tearing' down from the main road as Albert Beach proceeded to walk up Dere Street in the vicinity of Elishaw Bridge. This would, of course, fit perfectly with the version given by Evelyn Foster even down to the timing of just before 7 pm. However, Evelyn, who had the added benefit of sitting looking at a car in the beam of her full headlights, albeit for only a minute or so, stated that the car was 'closed' therefore, a saloon car. Albert Beach was a little more precise stating: 'I am absolutely certain this car was a two-seater.' He did, however, add that the car 'may have had a dickey seat.' This would appear to make the car more of a convertible or sports car rather than Evelyn's observed saloon. Albert Beach was also to make the observation that the car, 'seemed to be dark blue'. This also would fit in with Evelyn's observation that the car she saw was 'dark coloured'. To Evelyn, in the glare of her headlights, the car would appear to be either dark or light; it could have been a variety of colours within the blue, grey and black range. To Albert Beach, walking down a dark, country lane with no lighting at all plus the added handicap of being dazzled by the headlights of an oncoming car, that the car 'seemed dark blue' should be taken as highly suspect.

In support of the evidence of Albert Beach, was the evidence given to the police by Robert Townes. Robert Townes was a local gardener, who lived at Brownrigg Cottages, about a quarter of a mile from Elishaw road ends. At around 6-50 pm, Robert Townes was on Dere Street and saw Albert Beach walking along the road when he was passed by: 'A touring car with the hood up.' This was followed by the sighting of another car on the main Otterburn road; this was a saloon car which, appeared to stop some two hundred yards passed the Elishaw junction on the Otterburn side. After a short stop, the car moved on the direction of Otterburn, the car appearing to be a saloon. This second car was also seen by Albert Beach, at that time crossing a field in the angle of Dere Street and the Otterburn road. Albert Beach was to note that the saloon car, some two hundred yards from him, was about three hundred yards east of Elishaw Road Ends and travelling towards Otterburn.

Although Evelyn Foster was quite sure that the car she saw was 'closed', therefore a saloon, Albert beach was to note that it was a two-seater and Robert Townes that it was a touring car with the hood up. A touring or soft-top car, even with its hood up, could not be mistaken as a closed car. Even though the timing of the cars seems to place them at the same point as that seen by Evelyn, the description just does not match. Coincidence or not, these cars must have been two different cars. The other car, a saloon, seen on the Otterburn road by both Albert Beach and Robert Townes, must have been none other than Evelyn Foster's Hudson returning to Otterburn.

If there is one thing certain then it is that, if the man got into Evelyn's car then, at some time, he had to get out again. According to her statement, he got out after the car stopped outside the 'Kennels'. Arrangements had been made that Evelyn would pick him up at the bridge, next to the 'Percy Arms', after he had visited the 'Percy Arms' enquiring about a lift. Although there appeared to be more than a few people on the street that night, no one could definitely say that they saw the man. George Maughan, as we have seen, had Evelyn's Hudson in full view from the time it approached Otterburn until it stopped outside the 'Kennels'. Although, the time coincided with his arrival at that spot, George Maughan was to say: 'I saw no one get out.' George Maughan did however see a man, on the other side of the road, north side, near the Church gates. This man he did not recognise but it could not have been the man from Evelyn's Hudson that was still in motion at the time. As George Maughan approached the car, within four or five feet, he did notice that a woman was in the driving seat but, was unable to see if anyone else was in the car. Robert Luke, brother in law of Gordon Foster, came out of the Foster garage at 7 pm, crossing the road to the 'Kennels'. Although he saw and acknowledged George Maughan, he failed to see anyone else even though he had a good view down the street, at this point just short of three-hundred yards, as Evelyn had left the headlights of the Hudson turned on.

Between the Foster house and the 'Percy Arms' there appears to have been a lack of people to make any sightings at all. However, one person did see an unknown man. This was George Sinclair; manager of the Otterburn branch of the Co-Op. George Sinclair had been carrying out some stock checks and was working later than usual. Stepping out into the street at about 7 pm, he saw a strange man lurching outside the Post Office, a building next to the Co-Op. The man moved off hurriedly in the direction of the 'Percy Arms' as George Sinclair approached him. George Sinclair was to make a statement to the press: appearing under the heading: 'Mystery Stranger'. 'I met Mr George Sinclair, the manager of the local Co-operative Society, who is convinced that he saw a stranger in the village at the time Evelyn Foster was preparing her car for the journey from which she was to return to her deathbed. Here is his own statement. "No one he said will shake me in my opinion that the man I saw outside the Post Office shortly after seven o'clock was a stranger to Otterburn. The man was similar in build to the man described by Miss Foster in her statement and he was walking towards the bridge. It was so dark I could not see his face. I told the police officer that I had seen this man, and I was sure, that he was a stranger – you can always sense strangers in a village like this after dark. Why they did not call me to the inquest, I do not know.'[2] It is possible that this man was the same one that George Maughan had seen near the Church gates. The Church is almost opposite the Co-Op and the man could easily have crossed the street after he was seen by George Maughan. Using the statement of George Maughan, the man, whoever he was, could not have come from Evelyn's Hudson, at the time George Maughan passed him they were some thirty-four to thirty-five yards from the 'Kennels' and Evelyn's Hudson had not stopped yet. Even if the car had been stationary, George Maughan saw no one walking down the street even though he had a clear enough view.

Although Evelyn did not seek out the company of George Philipson for whatever reason, as she had promised her mother, George Philipson was out on the main street of Otterburn. He was to make a statement, as many did, via the press. He had visited the Garage where he learned, from whom no one knows that Evelyn was going on a journey. He then dashed out just in time to see Evelyn's Hudson disappear out of the village. He was in an agitated maybe distressed state; could this be the man seen by George Sinclair? George Sinclair was to admit that he could not see the man's face. That George Philipson did not acknowledge George Sinclair could simply be explained in the fact that Philipson was anxiously rushing to get to The 'Percy Arms' before Evelyn left: something he failed to achieve. George Philipson could also have been the man seen by Miss Mary Ferry in the vicinity of the 'Percy Arms'.

THE PERCY ARMS 1928

The man, according to Evelyn, was going to call at the 'Percy Arms' to enquire about a lift to Ponteland, had he done so, he would surely have asked anyone in the hotel, in turn they would surely have passed him on to John Scott, hotel chauffeur and barman. However, no one asked John Scott about a lift, in fact, John Scott had seen no person in the bar that was unfamiliar to him and he was to state: 'Anyone entering the door must pass me'. Added at the bottom of his statement, in ink, are words to the effect that not only did he not see Evelyn but, neither did he see a *strange* man. Likewise, Mrs Gladys Tatham saw no man in the lounge. However, a strange man had been seen in the vicinity of the 'Percy Arms'.

Miss Annie Carruthers, a schoolteacher at the village school at Elsdon, just under two miles to the east of Otterburn, was approaching Otterburn shortly after 7 pm when she was accosted by a man on the bridge over the Otter Burn. The man asked Miss Carruthers if she knew the time of the bus to Newcastle, Miss Carruthers, replied she did not but he could ask at the hotel. The man then became abusive and Miss Carruthers left him to it; not before she took note of his dress, however. The description by Miss Carruthers supports that of Evelyn Foster. Miss Mary Ferry, who is also teacher, albeit at Otterburn School, entered the Percy Arms. She had placed an order for her favourite sausages from Hexham, these were delivered to the Hotel by the Foster bus and Miss Ferry retrieved them from the Hotel reception. On leaving the Hotel and walking towards the bridge, Miss Ferry, noticed a man off to her right, beneath the trees. She looked once more but failed to recognise the man and picked up her pace as she crossed the bridge: she left no description of the man but, noted the time of 7-15 pm.

Using the times alone, the man who accosted Miss Annie Carruthers could not have been the man from Evelyn's taxi, he did not have the time to walk the almost three-hundred yards from her taxi, outside the 'Kennels' to the bridge just beyond the 'Percy Arms'. If he had done so, he would have had to pass George Maughan en route and this did not happen. George Maughan had had the taxi in view from around 7 pm when it was still on the road into the village. The man noted by Miss Mary Ferry could not be the *strange* man either, at this time, Evelyn's taxi was well on its way to Raylees Farm. It does appear a bit odd that, in so short a distance and an equally short period of time, a *strange* man was seen by four different people. In a small, tight-knit community like Otterburn, everyone is known by everyone else and that included the district for a few miles in either direction.

There now appears to be a gap in time before any other known reference to the man. The reference came by way of John Kennedy, a council road-mender from Kirkwhelpington. John Kennedy was passed by a north bound saloon car, travelling at 'high speed' on the Otterburn road, as we have already seen. Later, in the Coroners Court under questioning he was to further state: 'He seemed to be sitting more sideways than straight at the wheel.' Both of his statements in referring to a man, especially in the dark as well as in a car at 'high speed', appear to be highly fanciful to say the least. However, it is the only other reference to the man in the whole plot.

If the man was *invisible* then the *mystery* woman appears to be even more so. The only person recorded as seeing this woman at Elishaw Road Ends or anywhere else was Evelyn Foster. 'There was a woman in the driver's seat of the car' she was to state. As for the description of the car, she was also quite clear, describing its colour as 'dark' and the type as 'closed'. The only two witnesses to seeing any car on Dere Street were Albert Beach and Robert Townes, both witnesses being passed by a car and describing it as a two-seater or a touring car. Both of these descriptions are for a soft-top car therefore, differing from Evelyn's description of a saloon.

Where, Evelyn had said a woman was sitting in the driver's seat with probably another person in the front; neither Albert Beach nor Robert Townes could say who or how many were in the cars that they saw. A police statement was issued on 7 January in connection with this car. 'Will the party who were travelling south from Scotland in a motor-car and from which a man whom they gave a lift alighted at Elishaw Road Ends, north of Otterburn, about 6-30 pm, kindly communicate with the police.' Oddly the statement gives the wrong time being almost thirty minutes too early. Needless to say no one ever came forward.

According to Evelyn's story, the man had met the woman and at least one more man, in Jedburgh. Over tea, the man had informed the woman that he was on his way to Newcastle while the woman had said she was going to Hexham. A valid question would be why was the woman not willing to make a detour, not great, and take the man on to Ponteland? A probably more valid question would be, why did the woman not give him a lift right through to Hexham, if that was where she was going? From Hexham the man, would have had a reasonable choice of travelling by bus or train into Newcastle. The Coroner was later to use this same line of thought in the summing up at the inquest he spoke of the man: 'At Elishaw he appears to have been left with a definite uncertainty of being able to proceed from there to Newcastle by bus.' Rather than leave the man with some sort of transport she left him literally in the middle of the Northumberland Moors on a winter's night.

All we can glean from this is that, the woman did not want to take the man to Hexham for reasons she did not want the man to know. This leaves the possibility that she was not going there herself and had lied to the man about her destination or, there was no man and equally no woman either. That the woman did not wish to take the man beyond Elishaw has many possible answers and all would be conjecture without the evidence of the woman herself. However, on the possibility that Evelyn's story was true, that the woman was not seen beyond Dere Street would suggest that she had no reason to go further: she lived there. It is this theory, that the woman was local, that was upheld by local opinion.

The story we have is based on the evidence of Evelyn Foster alone, that Evelyn Foster had given a lift to a *strange* man who had been given a lift from Jedburgh. There is a possibility that the man lied to Evelyn as well in the first place. As this evidence by Evelyn is all we have it would be pure speculation to argue otherwise. The police issued a statement to the press as well as the radio in their attempt to get the person or persons to come forward; they never did. There are various arguments that can be put forward to explain the reason they did not come forward, one of these reasons, put forward by a crime reporter on the *Newcastle Journal,* is that, the man, as well as the other occupants, was a member of a gang.

This gang, argues the reporter, must have been on a 'job' in Scotland and were travelling back into England from some scene of crime hence the high speed of the car observed by Albert Beach as it travelled down Dere Street from Elishaw.[3] If this had been the case, why drop one of their members off at a remote road end on the Northumberland Moors? The organised crime theory just does not fit the story at all and it's hard to say why it was put forward at all without being a little unkind.

The fact that the mystery woman driver was of local origins was put forward by Goodman based on evidence put forward by some residents of Otterburn, among them a Mrs Dorothy Groves. Her father was William Blackham, Otterburn Schoolmaster, and she overheard him discussing the Foster case with a friend. Mr Blackham had pointed to a house, across the fields on Dere Street stating that was where the mystery woman lived. The woman seemingly, lived a double life and was in the habit of travelling to Jedburgh as well as having many male 'friends'. She was also known to be regularly in the clutches of various states of intoxication. The fact that the car, seen by Albert Beach and Robert Townes, vanished so quickly after turning down Dere Street was accounted for by the fact that the driver lived on Dere Street. The fact that she was going no further than Deere Street was the reason that she dropped the man off at Elishaw Road Ends.

After entering Dere Street, there are only two ways to leave it by road in the first few miles. This is the cross roads, some two and a half miles into Dere Street after Elishaw. In one direction the road goes to the small village of Bellingham while the other takes a one and a half mile detour to the south end of Otterburn. At around 6-50 pm, two men, a Mr Wallace and Mr Bell, set off on their bicycles on a journey from West Woodburn to Rochester by way of Dere Street, a total of some seven miles with Elishaw Road Ends at about five miles. No vehicle passed them on the whole of Dere Street and, if a car had turned off to either Bellingham or Otterburn, at the cross roads, they were close enough to have seen the lights. The only conclusion therefore, is that the car that entered Dere Street at Elishaw Road Ends and stopped somewhere along that first two and a half miles of Dere Street.[4]

On the surface, this all ties in with the statements of Evelyn Foster as well as the evidence of both Albert Beach and Robert Townes. It certainly explains how and why the car vanished so quickly backed up by the statements of Mr Wallace and Mr Bell. The car seen by Albert beach and Robert Townes was reported as going quite fast: *tearing* as he put it which at least implies it was going faster than would normally be expected on that road. As the roads were covered in frost as well as ice, surely, although the road had only one bend in it, this would point to someone with local knowledge of the road? The woman is described by Goodman only as Mrs X and she was known to have formerly owned a Ford car until replaced in late 1930 by a Morris.[5] Both Albert Beach and Robert Townes had identified the car that passed them as a 'soft-top'. Albert Beach gave it as a 'two-seater' with possible 'dickie' seat while Robert Townes described it as a 'touring' car. Only Albert Beach of the two stated that the car *seemed* to be dark blue. Of interest however, Albert Beach was to put forward that he *thought* the car could be a Morris Cowley; he just could not be certain. The Morris Cowley of around 1930 came in saloon and soft top as well as a two-seat soft top.

We also have a description of the car given by Evelyn Foster and, she was in a good position to view it for, as it sat squarely in the headlights of her Hudson. She was to state that the car at Elishaw Road Ends was a 'closed' car, therefore a saloon. However, she did state that it was dark coloured without venturing to name a colour. It should also be noted that, Evelyn, even though the car was well lit, did not recognise the car; not even the make. In pre World War Two Britain, cars were seen only as a necessity among those who could afford them. In rural Northumberland this was probably even more so. In the area of Otterburn, very few women owned or even drove a car. Apart from Evelyn Foster there were only two other women who owned or drove cars, as we have seen, in the immediate area.

Of those that did own or drive a car on a regular basis, Evelyn would surely have known most if not all, as she drove about the district in her taxi. Any woman would have been the focal point in gossip if they had a car, even more so if they bought a new one such is community gossip. The argument was put forward that Mrs X did not frequent Otterburn, travelling mainly to Jedburgh, Hexham and Newcastle. However, Evelyn travelled the roads on a regular basis and she was known to like a bit gossip with her passengers. A woman like Mrs X, living within such a short distance of Otterburn would have been known to Evelyn Foster if not, then her car certainly would. Part of the argument put forward by Goodman was based on the possibility that the *mystery* woman knew of Evelyn's taxi and knew it would be at Elishaw Road Ends at that time. If Mrs X knew that much then Evelyn Foster would certainly know Mrs X.

Using the timing of Mr Wallace and Mr Bell, cycling from West Woodburn to Rochester, they should have been near the Otterburn to Bellingham cross roads at around 7 pm. That they did not see any car headlights along the road, points to the fact that the car on Elishaw road, if you accept Evelyn's statement, had turned off the Elishaw road at some point. Although there is a rise in the road between the cross roads and Elishaw, any lights on that road would have been visible, even as a glare in the sky.

The Mrs X of Goodman's story was Mrs Charlotte Clark who was married to John Clark [6] of the family business of Clarks Thread Company later to be amalgamated with their rival Coats as Coats and Clark of Paisley, Scotland. The home of the Clark's was Troughend Hall some two miles from Elishaw road ends on the south side of the road.[7] If the car on the Elishaw road that night was the car of Mrs Clark then it would have been off the road within ten minutes of it having been seen by Albert Beach and Robert Townes. However, Troughend Hall stands on the highest part of that road, on top of a hill, the lights would have been seen for miles. According to Goodman, Mrs Clark (Mrs X) was visited by the police on 7 January, in connection with the car driven along the Elishaw road the previous night. Mrs Clark was indisposed due to a sudden attack of the flu: it's not known if the police ever returned to pursue their inquiry.

The mystery woman had only been seen by Evelyn Foster; in her statement, Evelyn only referred to her as: 'A woman was in the driver's seat.' From this, it is safe to assume that Evelyn did not recognise the woman, had she done so she would have said. Apart from Evelyn, the only other person to see the mystery woman was none other than the invisible man. Of those that saw her car or a car at that particular time, neither Albert beach nor Robert Townes had any idea if the driver was male or female. Although the police had visited various establishments in Jedburgh in the hope that someone could throw some light on the group, no one was prepared to come forward.

The same response came from Ben Prior of the 'Redesdale Arms' just south of Rochester and some one and a half miles from Elishaw Road Ends. However, Ben Prior was to state that three men were there on that night, leaving at around 7 pm they travelled south towards Otterburn in a dark coloured Essex car. The Essex was a similar car to the Hudson; could it be that this was the car seen by Albert Beach and Robert Townes on the Otterburn road? Lying only one and a half miles from the 'Redesdale Arms', the Essex would have passed Elishaw at around 7-10 pm however, after drawing a blank at Jedburgh and the 'Redesdale Arms' it would appear that the mystery woman was to remain untraceable.

That a local woman was involved in the events of 6 January and, that that woman was Mrs Clark who lived on Dere Street, really has to be pure speculation. The evidence against Mrs Clark is based on a second-hand account tinged, perhaps, with some local resentment for who knows whatever reason, was put forward by a Mrs Groves who had witnessed, clandestinely, her father William Blackham, Otterburn schoolmaster. William Blackham had pointed out the house, across the fields from Otterburn School, as being the home of the mystery woman; the house was Troughend Hall, clearly viewable from the Otterburn to Rochester road. There was no real evidence then and there certainly is none now.

The nearest we can get to apportioning blame is that the police called to interview her only to find she was indisposed with flu. Whether she had or not, the Police should have returned after a few days. Their lack of duty has only served to perpetuate the myth of the mystery woman. It is quite possible that Mrs Clark was innocent the events of that night however, once doubt has been set on course it is hard to remove and the myth of the mystery woman is set down in the history of the events of 6 January. This leaves her to disappear in the mists of time, an enigma within a mystery story.

The same cannot be said for the invisible man however. He too was only seen by Evelyn Foster and described in minute detail. So detailed that the police were driven to unleash the man's description on the public. This description was flashed, courtesy of the press, newspapers and radio, not only around the County but also the Country. The description was: 'Height five foot six inches, dark, slim build and wearing a bowler hat, dark (blue?) overcoat and suit.' In such a quiet backwater like Otterburn, there seems to have been an unusual number of *strange* men abroad. The statement of George Sinclair emphasises the *strange* man in their midst as does the statement of barman John Scott: having *strange man* added to the bottom of his statement in ink. An important point to remember is the fact that, the statements were made days after the event as well as days after the description of the man by the Police was issued. Which begs the question, were they influenced by the Police statement rather than the truth of what they actually saw?

Albert Beach also spoke of a man he met just outside Otterburn, going to describe him as a: 'short, thick set man with a long blue overcoat.' John Kennedy also seems to have been slightly influenced by the Police statement. He was to say a car passed him in which: 'I noticed that a man was driving, but saw no one else in the car: I am unable to say whether the driver wore a bowler hat or had any head covering.'

The statement issued by the police was to cause more panic amongst the public than almost anything else. On the morning after the event, John Orminston, an Otterburn blacksmith, was reported as seeing a *strange* man coming from the direction of Otterburn Tower. This building stands on the east side of the Percy Arms a short distance from the bridge over the Otter Burn; later to be used as the police Headquarters in Otterburn. The local press in the form of the *Evening World*, went so far as to suggest that the *strange* man had doubled back, after the events of the night before at Wolf's Nick and was hiding in Otterburn Tower or in the surrounding woodland. The police arrived and, after a detailed search was forced to admit the search had been fruitless and without success.

Away from the immediate area of Otterburn a young man of twenty-three or four had entered a Presbyterian Church in Gosforth during a service. Even though he was just in the ante room, the people inside the church somehow got word to those outside that a *strange* man was in the Church and the police were alerted. On attending the Church, the Gosforth police were to find only that the young man, well dressed, was only trying to obtain money for his fare home to Scotland. A mysterious car was reported in Fuse Hill Street, Carlisle and had been seen to be carrying three men. The car was eventually stopped by Sergeant Henderson in Botchergate, near the railway station. The three men had agreed to be questioned and, after giving a valid reason as to their whereabouts, were allowed to travel on their way. One man in Carlisle, a Mr David John Rammage, a boarder at a hotel in Lockerbie Road, had suspicions of a fellow boarder and alerted the police. On arrival at the hotel, the police could find no trace of the man in question. Similar cases were recorded in areas such as Alnwick and Morpeth, all involving young men wearing bowler hats and all without any eventual outcome.

While the story was to gain much publicity over the next few weeks, courtesy of the local press and much of it nothing more than pure speculation, it was the idea of the *strange* man that was to put the area on its guard. A strange man, after apparently committing a murder, was on the loose in the area. One newspaper was to report: 'I find among the country folk themselves there is a strong belief that the assailant is still at large in the district, although they do not believe he is a local man.' The same newspaper, the *Evening World* was to further state: 'In any case, there is a most uneasy feeling throughout the area, and cottage doors are being more securely bolted than ever.' Shepherds, farmers and anyone else who worked out in the open were to be on their guard. Mr M.C. Hutton, a shepherd of Belling Farm, Plashetts in the Kielder area, saw a man striding over the fells and alerted the police. Like most others, when the police arrived he had vanished. This area is now under the waters of the Kielder reservoir, if that was the man and he was later to succumb to the weather conditions, he will remain there, hidden forever. Stories such as this, although nothing ever came of them, caused many who had never even thought of security, to lock and bolt doors and, as one woman was reported to do, keep things such as knives beneath their pillow at night. Such was the power of thought brought about by the *invisible* man.

The question uppermost in the minds of many was; did he manage to evade those in search of him and eventually to escape the wild moors and fells or, did the moors eventually claim him as well? The *Newcastle Evening Chronicle* was to air this problem as well: 'Has the murderer of Evelyn Foster perished on the wild fells? Never before have I realised that within fifty miles of industrial Tyneside lies one of the wildest and most desolate areas of Great Britain. It may be days or weeks or even months before the body is found, but they feel confident that the wild Northumberland moors have claimed the murderer and his victim.'

According to the evidence of Evelyn Foster, the man was dressed, more or less like a city gent, a 'nut' as she was to put it. His clothes designed and more suited to a night on the town rather than nights on the wild moorland. The area around Otterburn is one of the bleakest outside the Highlands of Scotland. Even today parts of it are used for training purposes for the British forces. In the photographs of the period, showing Evelyn's Hudson, the ground appears to be covered by wild grass. However, these are tufts. To walk on the moor, these tufts have to be used almost as stepping stones over a river, to miss one invites a good soaking as between the tufts is wet bog. It would have been cold enough on that night in ordinary clothing, to be wet as well would make it ten times worse.

The weather of that night has to be taken into account. It was very cold with a severe frost and more than a hint of snow. Photographs taken on the following days show police officers wearing heavy coats, their collars pulled well up against the weather and this was during the day. On the night of the event, the moon rose at 6-29 pm and, although a full moon it was also a low one giving little light. It had waned by 10 pm. There would be very little light for anyone to traverse the moor considering they did not know the area.

It would perhaps help if we had some idea of the exact time of the fire. However, the nearest we can get is a statement made by Sidney Henderson, a shepherd who lived in the isolated cottage at Harwood Head. The cottage lies a mere half mile to the east of Winter's gibbet on the Elsdon to Morpeth road and some two miles directly across the moors to the north of Wolf's Nick. Sidney Henderson stated that the time was 8-45 pm when, he went on to say: 'I looked over the moor in the direction of the main road to Otterburn in the direction of Wolf's Nick I saw a fire which I thought was a car had caught fire on the main road. The fire was very bright.' Looking round again at 9 pm, he noticed that the fire was now going down. Returning along the same road at 10-45 pm he was to notice that no fire at all could now be seen and he had seen no person at all at either time. Oddly, the police were to pay little heed to the evidence put forward by Sidney Henderson.

As the case of Evelyn Foster began to wane the local press made valiant attempts to keep it alive. One way of keeping up the interest was to make references to the *invisible* man. Was he alive or dead? In fact, did he even exist in the first place? The *Newcastle Evening Chronicle* explained away the *invisible* man by the use of some lyrical prose and the use of many of the place names of the surrounding area adding little, if anything to the reality of the story. 'Right up the Otterburn road, over the Carter Bar, along the Jedburgh – Riccarton trail, which runs parallel to the border, and away down the line to Kielder and Plashetts and Falstone, the grim news has travelled.

It is known up Hunter's Burn, and the wild Loaning Burn; it is whispered up the Kennel Burn, even as far as the Cutty burn, which tumbles from its source in the Girdle Stone'.[8] The police investigating the case were also to put forward the idea that there may never have been a man in the first place. This was not met which much enthusiasm, as can be expected, in Otterburn. Others have since conjured up stories which include the *invisible* man's background before admitting, it is after all maybe just conjecture.

The question that remains, truth or not, is, was it possible for a man on the run to survive the wild terrain of the moors? As we have seen, the man was not dressed for outdoor activities and his clothing would give him little, if any protection against the severity of the winter night on the moorland terrain: maybe even more than one night. The moorland around Otterburn is however, virtually littered with a variety of hiding places that could be used for shelter. These range from former grand farm houses of their day to the lonelier, humble shepherds outpost. All maybe in a ruinous state, however, all could equally be used for shelter by a man on the run. As one old shepherd put it at the time, an aeroplane crashed in the area and it took them days to find it.

To look for one man in so hostile a landscape could prove almost impossible. It is conjecture but a man could have survived for quite a while on the moorland, if he had local knowledge as well as survival expertise. The same moorland could provide him with a food source. Alternately, this man walked away from a murder scene and vanished into the moorland mists as well as the mists of time, to remain, alive or dead, undetected. On the other hand, the man may never existed outside the realms of the imagination of Evelyn Foster.

In an attempt to resurrect the *invisible* man and put an end to the Evelyn Foster case by means of uncovering the *invisible* man, Jonathan Goodman, gave his readers Ernest Brown, a groom from Huddersfield. Ernest Brown had had an affair of sorts with the wife of his employer, Frederick Morton.[9] Some twenty months after the death of Evelyn Foster, Ernest Brown shot Frederick Morton in the chest with one shot from a shotgun before proceeding to place the body of Morton in the driver's seat of his own car then setting fire to it. In an attempt to justify his case against Ernest Brown, Goodman points to the fact that Brown was born in Huddersfield with part of his childhood spent in Byker, in Newcastle's east end: therefore solving his accent. It was; 'Like Tyneside – not broad Tyneside but north-country'. As a groom, Brown was always well dressed and part of the 'uniform' of a groom was a bowler hat. This also ties in with the description of her attacker given by Evelyn Foster: 'He was a bit of a nut' The word 'nut' is spelt this way in the various reports but some later writers refer to it as 'Knut'. As a groom, to a man in the cattle business, Ernest Brown was known to have travelled widely and, in particular within the northern counties. Could he have been in Jedburgh on 6 January 1931? No one knows.

The main point in Goodman's argument takes place in Armley Gaol, Leeds. It was there on 6 February 1933, that Ernest Brown faced the hangman. His last words were to be to the prison chaplain. On being asked if he had anything to say, Ernest Brown is reported as saying either: 'Ought to burn' or 'Otterburn'. It should be remembered that Ernest Brown was talking through a mask and certainly would not be in a mood for chat anyway. The previous criminal record of Ernest Brown was known to have been for drunkenness and theft. Once a thief, always a thief the saying goes and the *invisible* man was not a thief, having left money, although not much, at the crime scene if, of course, he had been there at all. Only two men had knowledge of what Ernest Brown had said on the scaffold and one of those was hanged. The other, the chaplain, only 'thinks' that was what Brown said which is hardly proof positive for the closure of a murder case. However, it is a fact that various people who have related to the story of Evelyn Foster, have seized on the last utterances of Ernest Brown, blown them up out of al proportion and passed them off as fact, something they were not. All this has done is to perpetuate a myth. To further muddy the waters, there is a hamlet in Yorkshire that also bears the name Otterburn. Therefore, even the name, Otterburn is not proof that Ernest Brown meant Otterburn, Northumberland.

NOTES.

1) Statement given by Evelyn Foster via her mother. Coroner's report COS/3/54/1 Northumberland Archives Woodhorn.

2) *Evening World* issue February 6. 1931.

3) Julian Symons 'A Reasonable Doubt' "The Invisible Man" The Cresset Press 1960 P 193.

4) Jonathan Goodman. 'The Burning Of Evelyn Foster' David & Charles 1977. P 132 – 135.

5) Jonathan Goodman p132 states that the Morris owned by Mrs 'X' was a saloon.

6) John and Charlotte Clark were recorded as living at Troughend Hall from at least 1920. They were listed in Kelly's Directory, 1921, as living there. Although John Clark was thought to have connections with Clark's thread company, he was also a farmer (gentleman variety). The small Troughend Tofts Farm was his. He is listed in various directories as having John Thomson as his farm bailiff. It is also known that John Clark was an air raid warden for Troughend during the Second World War. John and Charlotte Clark moved to nearby Dunns houses, a mere quarter of a mile from Troughend Hall c 1938.

7) Troughend Hall was built near the original foundations of a former Pele Tower. The Land, and later the Hall, was in the possession of the Reed family. A farming family by the name of Hall lived in Troughend Hall from at least 1851; various farming families lived there in later years. Lechie appears to have been the last farmer before John Clark took over. From the late 1930s, the Hall or at least parts of it, was rented out.
Plans to demolish Troughend Hall were passed in 1952. A photograph of Troughend Hall dates from 1956, the year it is thought that it was finally demolished.

8) *Newcastle Evening Chronicle* issue January 13, 1931.

9) Goodman ibid p 139 – 144.

CHAPTER SIX

THE INQUEST: A BATTLE OF WILLS

The inquest on the death of Evelyn Foster had been set to begin on Monday 2 February at 10-30 am: the venue was to be, as in the earlier inquest, the War Memorial Hall on the main street of Otterburn. All decorations and bunting left over from the Christmas festivities, and still in evidence at the previous inquest, had now been removed. The Coroner, Mr Philip Mark Dodds, His Majesties Coroner for South Northumberland, had arrived early at the War Memorial Hall, half an hour before the inquest was set to begin. The Special correspondent for The *Evening World* was to say that, he had been informed, by the Coroner, that the hearing would last for two days, it would then be adjourned and one of the main witnesses, Professor Stuart McDonald, would not be appearing until Thursday. The jury, as previous, would be made up of nine men, all of whom had known Evelyn Foster well. This could well be looked upon as being biased towards Evelyn Foster; should a jury be impartial? Reports were to say that there were surprisingly very few local people in the 'War Memorial Hall' and, of those that were there, many had walked miles over the hills and fells to be there. Captain

Fullarton James and the police contingent were also to arrive early, arriving shortly after Mr P.M. Dodds.

The Foster's, Margaret, Joseph and son Gordon, were to arrive at the 'War Memorial Hall' just prior to the beginning of proceedings. Margaret Foster, small and dumpy, was dressed in black while Joseph wore a dark suit and sported a bowler hat. The Fosters were to sit apart, almost aloof, from the rest of the witnesses, sitting near a large, paper-strewn, table. The police contingent also sat near a table with Superintendents Spratt and Thomas Shell and other police officers, in descending rank sitting near. With a slight gap in between the groups, from those taking part and those who weren't, sat the Chief Constable of Northumberland Constabulary, Captain Fullarton James and his deputy, Superintendent James McGilvray Tough. That this inquest was not just to be a straight forward hearing was shown in the fact that both parties, the police and the Fosters, had legal representation. Representing the police was Mr Thomas Hedley Smirk while his opposite number, representing the Fosters, was Mr Ernest Bates.

Coroner Dodds

At 10-30 am precisely, the formal proceedings got under way with Mr Dodds opening with a statement, or a broadside, depending on which side you represented. Mr Dodds was to point out that all statements were to be admitted as evidence, a veiled swipe at Evelyn Foster's statement as given by her mother, Mr Dodds went on to warn the jury: 'I have to impress on you that you must not take that statement as evidence of fact but as a line of inquiry to see if the evidence given, even though circumstantial, substitutes a statement.' If the jury, all men, who knew Evelyn, could be seen as being biased to Evelyn Foster then, the statement by Mr Dodds, could be seen as being biased towards the police. In effect what Mr Dodds was saying was, Evelyn Foster, was not innocent until proven guilty but, guilty until being proved innocent.

The first witness called was to be Margaret Foster, mother of the deceased. One of the first queries Mr Dodds was seeking an answer to was the reason as to why Mrs Foster was asking the questions at the bedside of her dying daughter. 'Did you voluntarily ask your daughter questions or did the police suggest you did?' She replied that as she sat nearest her daughter at her bedside, then she should ask the questions. Margaret Foster then related, clearly and with precision the story of the events of the night of 6 February as related to her by Evelyn beginning with her first encounter with the man at Elishaw Road Ends. He had said: 'He was trying to telephone from an AA box.' Mr Dodds wanted to how clearly Evelyn was capable of thinking and talking on that night. 'During the time she was making these statements to you, did she appear to be perfectly clear in what she was saying?'

THE KENNELS 1931

'Oh yes, she knew quite well what she was saying.'

'She seemed perfectly lucid and sensible about everything?'

'Yes. When Dr Miller came she apologised and said she was sorry to have brought him out on such a night.' Also in need of some explanation were Evelyn's business affairs, Mr Dodds perhaps approaching the theory, advanced by the police, that Evelyn had been the cause of the events of that night. 'Do you know if Evelyn had any worries at all: I know she had some worries about business?' That last suggestion appeared to prick the so far strong armour of Margaret Foster into a retaliatory response as she answered: 'What worries about business? Only about keeping books up to date and such things.'

It was now the turn of police representative Mr Thomas Hedley Smirk, to question the witness. He seized on the reason as to why

Evelyn Foster had failed to take along George Philipson, her friend, on that last fateful journey. Margaret Foster agreed that she had asked her daughter to take along George Philipson but Evelyn had failed to do so. Mr Smirk was to point out that Evelyn's only excuse, for not taking Philipson was that she had not seen him. Her sister, Margaret, had seen Philipson on the street only a short time after she had left; in fact, he had been close enough to see her car disappear out of the village. Mrs Foster agreed that this was so,

THE FOSTERS ARRIVE AT THE INQUEST

however, she was to state, that it had occurred to her later: 'That Evelyn would not have liked going to his lodgings.' Mr Smirk then referred to an earlier question, already addressed by the coroner, and asked again by him, Smirk, as if looking for vindication that the police were not guilty in any way: 'Were the particulars given by your daughter voluntary or in answer to questions? Mrs Foster replied in a matter of fact way: 'I asked her questions and she kept answering. My daughter made the statements herself.'

Mr Dodds now reverted back to Evelyn's journey and her identification of Mr Kirsopp Reed's car. Mrs Foster was to reply: 'Evelyn said she was not quite sure where she passed Mr Kirsopp Reed's car, but thought it was somewhere about Capheaton.' Asked about the assault that took place against her daughter, Mrs Foster went on: 'She was not sure whether her daughter said the man hit her again before they got to Wolf's Nick. 'Her impression was that the man did not change seats, but sat close beside Evelyn in order to keep his hand on the steering wheel'. Mr Dodds then asked if the car had actually stopped on the road. 'Yes. She said the car stopped on top of the hill at Wolf's Nick.'

Did you ask her if he interfered with her?' She stated that she had asked Evelyn that and her reply was: 'Yes mother.'

Making sure of the clarity of his question, Mr Dodds was to ask: 'Was any other words other than interfered used by you in your questioning of Evelyn?'

'No. I don't think so.'

'But you meant whether he had indecently assaulted her?'

'Yes.' Mrs Foster went on to state that Evelyn said she had fought for her life and, that the man had taken something out of his pocket, a bottle or tin, and threw it over her. Mr Smirk was now to ask: 'When you asked her if he had interfered with her, you meant had he outraged her?'

'Yes.'

With the questioning of Mrs Foster, by Mr Smirk, now at an end, Mr Dodds asked her if she could identify some pieces of Evelyn's clothing, some of it in bottles and all of it charred to some extent. Among the pieces were bits of her scarf and pieces of her skirt as well as her purse. Mrs Foster looked at them, merely nodding to confirm that she recognised them. At this point, the pressure finally got to Mrs Foster and she broke down. Leaving the witness chair, she turned her head to the wall and burst into tears. Mr Dodds then called on a constable to bring Mrs Foster a glass of water and escort her back to her seat, a female friend of hers also helped, and she settled beside Joseph and Gordon Foster.

With the evidence of Mrs Foster completed, attention shifted to other witnesses. The next two being, John Robson, a bus driver for the Foster's and Robert Harrison, also a bus driver for the Tait Motor Company. The evidence of John Robson was significant as he was the last person to see Evelyn's Hudson and, also, he gave a positive time; 7-22 pm at Raylees Farm. In effect, the statement by John Robson was to prove the evidence of witness Robert Harrison as of no use at all. At the time Evelyn was seen at Raylees Farm, Robert Harrison was leaving Knowesgate, some six miles south at 7-30 pm.

All the focus was now to be shifted back to the Foster's as the next witness was to be Joseph Foster. The first part of Joseph Foster's evidence was almost a retelling of the evidence of his wife, merely stating that Evelyn came home from Rochester and that he, Joseph Foster, had worked out a price for taking a man to Ponteland. He had only heard her, Evelyn, tell her mother: 'That she was having the car filled up with petrol.' He only glimpsed Evelyn as she passed through and was not to see her again until she was brought home after being found at Wolf's Nick. Joseph Foster was to say: 'I went out to the bus to receive her. Evelyn asked for a drink and I took her some coffee while she was inside the bus.' Coffee does appear to be an odd drink to give anyone suffering from burns. Firstly, there must have been some haste to get Evelyn from the bus into the house. Joseph, however, spent that time making a cup of coffee. Secondly, Evelyn had been seen by Cecil Johnstone, licking the frosted grass, at Wolf's Nick, in an effort to quench her thirst: a glass of water would have seemed a more appropriate drink.

Mr Dodds, opening his questioning, wanted to know when Joseph Foster had first heard the story of Evelyn taking a man to Newcastle, this should have been Ponteland. Joseph Foster was to reply: 'Her mother told me about it after Evelyn had left.' To which Mr Dodds replied: 'Very well, I will take your answer for it.' It would appear, from this answer that the Coroner was only reluctantly accepting Joseph Foster's answer. Mr Dodds was to now move his questioning into the area of Evelyn Foster's finances as well as her position in the business. Joseph Foster was to briefly describe Evelyn's Hudson stating that: 'It was a Hudson Super Six of over twenty-nine horsepower and it was a fast car. It was fitted with a luggage chest to the rear of the car and this chest was generally kept unlocked. Inside the chest was kept a two-gallon petrol tin which Evelyn used to carry extra petrol for emergencies, and this was normally kept wrapped in a sack. The car, he stated, was in perfect working order and the brakes were good. He was then asked by the Coroner if the petrol can was sealed in any way to which he answered: 'Well, it had a piece of wire on it and it seemed to be intact.' Joseph Foster did not elaborate on the wire fastening, it could be that it was some sort of spring-wire fastener, neither was he asked when the wire was 'intact'; it certainly was not when inspected at Wolf's Nick. When questioned by the Coroner about the purchase of the car, Joseph Foster was to reply: 'The car was bought about fourteen months ago for £200 odd, [1] I don't actually know.' However, Mr Dodds was not to be put off on this point as he asked: 'Can you find out and tell me later?' Joseph Foster replied: 'Yes'. Joseph Foster was also to point out that Evelyn's work-day consisted, as well as her taxi business, of clerking, attending to the house and other domestic duties.

Returning to the petrol tin, Mr Dodds, wanted to know what kind it was to which Joseph Foster replied that: 'The petrol can normally carried in Evelyn's car, was a 'Pratt's' can,' (the can found at the crime scene was a 'Shell' can) Mr Dodds went on to ask: 'When did you last see this can?' To which Joseph was to reply: 'About ten days before the tragedy.' From this exchange, it appears to be odd that Joseph Foster, his business lying in the motor trade, did not know the exact price Evelyn had paid for her car. It was bought second-hand and it would have been reasonable to expect that Joseph or his son Gordon, played some part in inspecting it before the car was bought. It would also have been reasonable to surmise that there would have been some discussion over a price for the car.

As the car was garaged in the Foster garage as well as being maintained there, Joseph Foster must surely have noted the type of petrol can carried in the car. However, Evelyn seemed to carry out the normal filling and checking of petrol. The fact remains that Joseph Foster had not seen the 'Pratt's can for at least ten days; in that time Evelyn could well have replaced the 'Pratt's' can for a 'Shell' can at any time. Even more so if she had sold that can of petrol to some stranded motorist while out on a trip. The last witnesses of the day were to be, Cecil Johnstone, Thomas Rutherford and Thomas Vasey all of their evidence was to be as in their statements and the inquest came to a close for the day.

The second day of the inquest was to open with the absence of the Foster family; they were to turn up later. A main focal point of the day was once again to be Joseph Foster who was to be recalled to answer questions of Evelyn Foster's finances, in particular her running costs and expenses of the taxi business: information Joseph had failed to produce on the first day. However, first occupant of the witness chair was to be John Kennedy, road mender of Knowesgate. It was John Kennedy who had witnessed a fast-moving car travelling north towards Otterburn on the night of 6 January.

John Kennedy was to state that, while he was walking home from Kirkwhelpington to Knowesgate, he had left Kirkwhelpington at around 8 pm and was about ten minutes into his journey, when he was passed by three motor cars. Two of these motor cars were travelling south while the third was travelling north towards Otterburn. It was the third car, being driven towards Otterburn that interested the coroner's hearing, especially the police and Mr Smirk. This car, some had suggested, could be Evelyn's Hudson returning from Belsay, if it had been that far at all of course. Mr Dodds was to ask John Kennedy to describe the car he saw. 'It was a dark saloon and my attention was drawn to it because it was being driven so fast. It was a moonlight night, and I could see that there was a man driving the car.' He went on to state that the number 1 and 3 were in the registration number but not in sequence. After giving his evidence to the coroner, John Kennedy was then faced with Mr Smirk and he could be forgiven for thinking that, rather than being a witness at an inquest hearing, he was on trial himself.

THOMAS H. SMIRK

Mr Smirk was to wonder why John Kennedy was to note one car's number and not the others as that one car with the numbers 1 and 3, could well have been Evelyn's car, the number of which was, TN 8135. Mr Smirk was to open with: 'Did you notice the numbers of the other two cars?' At this time John Kennedy appeared quite confident as he replied: 'I cannot tell you any of the numbers of the first car, but I remember the last three numbers of the second car were either 333 or 000.' Mr Smirk, for some reason not really clear, asked John Kennedy if he knew a man called William Herdman for he drove a car with the registration number BR 6123, Mr Herdman was a local farmer who was also at Kirkwhelpington that night. 'Yes' was the reply. Mr Smirk had been hoping to try and confuse John Kennedy with the numbers 1 and 3. However, before the question could be asked, John Kennedy supplied the answer: 'It was not that number because in the number I saw the figures 1 and 3 was together.' Obviously some were not paying full attention as John Kennedy had told the coroner that the numbers 1 and 3 were not in sequence; somehow it flew past without notice. Mr Smirk had pointed out that the number of Evelyn Foster's Hudson was TN 8135. Before Mr Smirk could ask the question, John Kennedy pointed out that, the car that passed him that night was not the car of Mr Herdman. Of that he was sure: 'Mr Herdman would not travel at such a furious pace.' John Kennedy, whether he knew it or not had supplied more evidence that the car he had seen could be that of Evelyn Foster.

After being somewhat sidetracked over the registration number of the car, Mr Smirk shifted up a gear as he focussed on the driver of that car. He opened with: 'You can say definitely that a man was driving the car?'

'I can. With the reflection from the road and the moonlight, I got a silhouette of the driver.' Mr Smirk then went on to question John Kennedy closer about the actual appearance of the driver: wanting to know the details: 'Could you see how the driver was dressed?'

'No. I could only see his face, above the face seemed to be shrouded in shadow.' Mr Smirk seemed to cast some doubt on this evidence of a man in a fast car, in the dark being identified or, just his face identified. John Kennedy, however, had no doubts and wished to force home his answers: 'I can positively swear a man was driving that car.' Aware that he was not going to shake the evidence of John Kennedy on the driver of the car, Mr Smirk, shifted focus to the following day: 'You were at the scene of the fire the following day and you saw the burned car?'

'Yes'.

'Did you then mention to the police that you had seen a car the previous night?'

'Well'.

Somewhat aggressively Mr Smirk went on: 'I do not want an explanation. Did you?'

'I cannot be sure.'

'I suggest that you never mentioned it until the police approached you about it ten days later.'

'I was rather under the impression I mentioned it to the constable on duty.'

'You think you did?'

'I am very hazy.'

'I suggest you never mentioned it?'

'It is possible.'

Mr Smirk had set out to prove that though there was a query over whether John Kennedy had seen Evelyn's car or not, it was up to him to prove that he had not. In the event, he cast doubt over all the evidence produced by John Kennedy. In defence of John Kennedy, he had begun his evidence with confidence, both in his timing and in his observation not only of the car but also the numbers 1 and 3. On his description of the driver, he may have been carried away: in reality, all he could see was a piece of face between hat and collar, caught by a reflection, presumably of dashboard lights, and the moonlight. In effect, he could not prove if it was a man or woman at all; it could well have been either. He then went on to stumble over the details of the next day and, in the end, allowed Mr Smirk to just stop short of calling him a liar. He stated that he spoke to a constable at Wolf's Nick: Constable Francis Sinton was on duty there from 6-30 am. Thereafter, there were various constables on duty until the arrival of Inspector Russell at 3-30 pm.[2]

William Herdman, a local farmer, was to be the next witness, seemingly with no other purpose than to discredit the evidence of John Kennedy. Kennedy had stated that the fast-moving car had passed him at about 8-10 pm, in the direction of Otterburn. Mr Herdman was to state that he left Kirkwhelpington at around 8-10 pm and arrived home, at Bellingham, some four and a half miles away, at 8-30 pm. His speed during the trip was given as a stately 13 – 14 mph and should have passed John Kennedy along the route, shortly after the time Kennedy saw the fast moving car. However, at a speed
of 13 -14 mph, Herdman could hardly be accused of travelling fast. Both men knew each other which raises the question, why did Herdman not stop to offer Kennedy a lift on so cold a night? This was answered by Herdman who went on to state: 'I have no recollection of seeing any vehicle or foot passenger.' The evidence given by John Kennedy was certainly discredited to say the least.

Walter Smith Beatie was next on the witness stand but only to reinforce his original statement that, he saw nothing moving at Wolf's Nick. As Evelyn Foster had stated that she heard a car pull up, followed by a whistle, it was more than likely that it was Beatie's car: as to the whistle, it could have been his brakes but he was unaware of any whistling from his brakes.

He was replaced on the witness stand by Gordon Foster and gave evidence as his written statement. Mr Smirk was to ask about the Hudson being in or out of gear and how the car had been handled, at Wolf's Nick as well as in the garage on its return. Gordon Foster was to reply: 'I could not get the gear out at first, it was in low gear. I released the gear but put it back in the position in which I found it when we got back to the garage. Police officers Fergusson, Proud and Turnbull all gave evidence in accordance with their statements. Inspector Russell was also to give his evidence as in his statement, informing the coroner that he had taken detailed measurements and observation of the car on his arrival at Wolf's Nick. The inquest was then adjourned for two hours and it was announced that Joseph Foster would be recalled.

When the inquest resumed it was to focus on the finances of Evelyn Foster and the lack of information provided by Joseph Foster, in connection with those finances. The coroner opened with: 'I think when you were last examined you said that your daughter's business was carried out on her own. Can you tell me what her earnings were? Mr Foster was to reply: 'I'm afraid I cannot at the moment. A book was destroyed in the car.' With some amazement, Mr Dodds was to continue: 'She would hardly carry an account book in her car surely?'

X MARKS THE SPOT WHERE THE HUDSON CAME TO REST

'Well, as a rule she did.'

'So you have no information on that then. Can you give me her bank balance?'

'Her bank balance at Lloyds Bank, Bellingham, was £84 – 10.' Mr Bates now intervened and pointed out that Evelyn Foster, had, in fact, £481-4-8 in her Lloyds Bank account with a further £8-5-4 in her Post Office account.[3] Acknowledging that fact, Mr Dodds moved on in an attempt to get at Evelyn's finances: 'What was the licence duty on the car?'

'She took out a licence for a hackney.' The licence was then produced for the coroner's perusal, showing that the cost of the licence was £3-6 to be paid quarterly and it was registered in the name of Evelyn Foster. The car insurance policies were then submitted to the coroner by Mr Bates, who also dealt with the finances of the Foster's. After studying the two policies, Mr Dodds observed: 'This policy, one you referred to as being insurance for a total of £400, but it appears to be a policy which covers risk in the motor garage and repair shop against fire.' Probing the document further Mr Dodds was to note: 'I see this policy is taken out in your name and not Evelyn's?'

'Well, we have a floating policy; we get it at a much cheaper rate through insuring it in my name. The insurance people understand it was Evelyn's car.' Probing even further, Mr Dodds continued: 'Is this the only policy you have against fire?'

'Yes.'

The second policy was to show that the car was insured against anything that might happen out on the road. Mr Smirk then scrutinised the accident policy before handing it back to the coroner with the words: 'It has no bearing on the matter.' To which Mr Dodds replied: 'Quite right, it states that the policy covers the third party risks, fire, theft or accident up to £1,000 on any car up to thirty horse power, Evelyn's Hudson was just under that at 29.4 horse power, up to the value or £700 maximum.

Before the day's proceedings came to an end, juryman, Mr Baxter wanted John Kennedy recalled to answer questions on the seated figure in the car. It was Mr Smirk that he had to face once more. 'Was there anything to suggest that between the man who was driving this car and the offside of the car there was a woman?

'I cannot say. I saw no woman.'

'In a statement you have made you said that there was a 1 and 3 among the letters. Can you say if these were the last?'

'No, but they were placed together.'

'Do you now say, having regard to the refreshing of your memory from these proceedings, that you did not know how the 1 and the 3 were placed?' However, John Kennedy was not to be put off and answered: 'In my statement to the police I made a stipulation that the

1 and the 3 were together.' With that the day's proceedings came to an end and the hearing was adjourned until Thursday 5 February.

Thursday 5 February was set to be the final day of the inquest: the day that all would be revealed, was it murder or did Evelyn set fire to the car herself? Before the inquest even got under way there was drama outside the hearing. Captain Fullarton James and his group were travelling to Otterburn from Police Headquarters at Morpeth, when the car they were travelling in overturned on the ice-covered road near Wolf's Nick. All the occupants managed to struggle free of the overturned car by means of the side windows. They then set about rocking the car back and forth, managing to get it back upright, then proceeded with a bit more care to Otterburn arriving late at the War Memorial Hall, and they unflappably took their seats.

First witness of the day, Dr Edward McEachran was already giving his evidence which remained the same as his earlier statement to the police. The cause of death, he had given as, death due to shock after severe burning. He did, however, state that Evelyn Foster had been completely lucid and aware of what was going on around her. He was also to emphasise, as in his statement, that Evelyn said she heard the petrol tank explode.

When Dr Edward McEachran left the stand he was replaced with the man most people had come to hear: Professor Stuart McDonald the pathologist; Professor of Pathology at the University of Newcastle upon Tyne. There had been much speculation and rumour about the Evelyn Foster case since 7 January, the day after the alleged attack. Had she been raped, had she been battered in her own car, had she been the victim of some mad psychotic, who may still be on the loose, and who had later set fire to her car in order to destroy all evidence? These and many more were the rumours that were in circulation, not only throughout the County of Northumberland, but throughout the Country. On this day, 5 February, all these questions would finally be answered including, hopefully the most vital question of all, was it murder or was the result self inflicted?

Professor McDonald, who had been assisted in the post mortem by Dr Stuart McDonald Jr, was to read out from his report the gruesome details of the post mortem and the last details of the life of Evelyn Foster. He would deal with the description of the burns to the body of Evelyn Foster before moving on to the evidence for the assault on her leaving until the end, any details of sexual attack. The whole hearing now held its breath as Prof McDonald began.

'The most severe burns were situated on the front of the middle portion of the body, on the front and inner aspect of the upper part of both thighs and, to a lesser extent over the lower portion of the flanks on both sides. On the back of the body in this neighbourhood there was also extreme burning extending from a transverse line just below the middle of the buttocks downwards and becoming continuous with the burned areas of the inner aspect of the thigh. There was also severe burning of the face. The fire had started in front of the body and, generally speaking, diminished in both upwards and downwards directions though both the hands and the face were severely burnt. The left foot and ankle were practically free from evidence of burning, but the right ankle and the top of the right foot showed superficial burning and blistering. There was evidence of burning as high as the breast; above the breast there were definitely localised areas of burning, the largest being about the size of a half crown piece. [4]

The distribution of the burned area on the lower portions of the buttocks and the absence of burning on the upper portions of the buttocks suggested that the deceased had been sitting during some period of the burning. Further, the absence of burning on the upper part of the chest, below the chin, together with the burning of the face, might be accounted for by a bending forward of the head.

The second part of his report was directed to any other injuries such as suggested by punching, slapping or nipping. 'No external marks suggesting injury apart from the burns were found on any other part of the body, but over the burned area superficial injuries or scratches could not possibly have been recognised. On the head, there was no wound of the scalp and there was no evidence of superficial or deep bruising.' The next part of the report concentrated on any possibility of sexual attack. 'I examined the deceased for evidence of sexual interference but came to the conclusion that she was virgo intact; there was no evidence of violation.'

Professor McDonald, stated that amongst the evidence that he had studied there had been suspected blood. A mudguard, a door handle and a piece of heather: there was a piece of chipped paint on the mudguard, this had been chipped for a while, and had left a rusted area suggestive of blood. However, it was not to be and Professor McDonald concluded: 'There was no blood present on either of the mudguards, the door handle or the heather.' He also stated that certain pieces of clothing had been tested: 'Certain places suggested that certain portions of clothing had contained some inflammable substance.' After finishing reading his report, Professor McDonald was asked by Mr Dodds what he had found on his trip to Wolf's Nick. The Professor was to reply that he had found two pieces of skin lying on the ground; one piece was identified as coming from the palm of a hand, the other he could not identify from which part of the body it had originated.

Mr Dodds now sought to get to the bottom of any bruising that would prove that Evelyn had been assaulted or not. Even though it was asked as a question, it was put in a way that suggested Mr Dodds already knew the answer. If that question had been put to any less a person than Professor McDonald it could have been looked upon as a leading question. 'So far as the bruising or slapping of the face is concerned; I suppose there was none of that?'

'I saw no evidence of it.'

'If it had been at all severe you could have done?'

'Any severe bruising I could have found.'

Seemingly determined to find proof that there had been no form of attack, Mr Dodds continued: 'There was no sign of any blow or injury which would have been strong enough to have stunned her?'

'As I pointed out in my report: I could not find anything superficial, I could not find any deep bruising.'

'If the girl was knocked or stunned you would have found some evidence?'

'I think we might reasonably expect it.'

Mr Dodds then shifted his questioning to looking for some evidence of sexual attack on Evelyn Foster. The answer to her mother's question: 'Had she been interfered with?' had brought an affirmative response from Evelyn: 'Yes'. Again my Dodds was to set a question that looked as if he already had the answer: 'Of signs of outrage there were none?'

'None whatever.' Mr Dodds then referred to the statement of Margaret Foster, quoting her daughter of which Professor McDonald had no knowledge of until that day. Pointing out that Evelyn had said that the man continually 'nipped' her arms: 'Was there any sign of this?'

There was no sign whatever of any nipping.' Mr Dodds then attempted a description of various scenarios in a veiled attempt to suggest that Evelyn herself had started the fire. 'Assuming no burning took place in the way the girl alleged, assuming the car was standing where you saw it, and she put some petrol into the back of the car and then set fire to it, with one leg on the running board and the other on the step of the car, could the flames have come back to the girl?'

'I think that is possible.' Mr Dodds went on to enquire about the localisation of the burns: 'Would it suggest that someone had poured something over her to increase the inflammability?' Professor McDonald replied short and to the point: 'Yes'.

Mr Smirk was then to ask Professor McDonald: 'It has been stated that Miss Foster was outraged?'

'Yes'.

'She was not?'

'That is so.'

Mr Smirk was then to move on to question about Evelyn Foster having been struck by the man, her mother said she had been struck twice, knocking her about and nipping her: was there evidence of that?'

'I found no such thing.' [5]

The Foster's sat listening to the evidence during this period. Mrs Foster sat impassive as she had been throughout most of the hearing while Mr Foster, showing the most anxiety, had his arm around his wife, gazing mainly at the floor and occasionally taking out a handkerchief to wipe his eyes. However, Mr Dodds was still looking for ways and means on how the burns could have been produced. 'The burns could have been gained in various ways?'

'Yes. I have suggested that during a certain period of the burning Miss Foster was sitting.'

Sensing a possible lead, Mr Dodds asked: 'Not necessarily in the car?'

'No, But on some straight edge.' Professor McDonald was attempting to clarify, that the burns could have occurred not just while sitting on a seat, such as the rear seat of the car, they could have also occurred if Evelyn Foster had been sitting on the running board of the car: a straight edge.

PROF MACDONALD

Mr Bates was then to ask about Evelyn Foster's scarf, asking if it had shown signs of being dragged from Evelyn Foster's neck: 'Was it tested for anything such as straining or pulling or, was it tested only for burning?'

'We examined it all ways.'

Juryman Rev Brierley was then to ask Professor McDonald about the claims that Evelyn Foster had been struck about the face, for example: 'Was there any facial discolouration?'

'I found no discolouration. There was no evidence of bruising really.'

Mr Bates, who had not been the greatest of questioners, then asked what surely must be the stupidest of questions: 'But that does not prove that bruising did not take place? In reply he was to receive the forthright answer: 'Well, the only proof of bruising I know, is finding evidence of it.' Another juryman then asked about disappearing bruising; bruising that could have taken place during an attack then disappeared before the body was examined. Professor McDonald was then to reply: 'It was not possible for slight bruising to have disappeared between the time of death and when I examined the body.' With that question answered, Professor McDonald departed the witness stand.

The next witness was also eagerly awaited, motor engineering expert William Jennings. Mr Jennings described what he had seen at Wolf's Nick; describing how the car had left the road at an angle of forty-five degrees and then travelled across the moor until it came to a stop. After a detailed inspection of the Hudson, he was satisfied that: 'The fire did not result from a leaking petrol pipe, short circuit or a silencer explosion.' He went on: 'I am strongly inclined to think that some agency outside the car itself has been the cause of the fire, but whether an inflammable liquid or other material had been the medium there was no evidence to say.' Mr Dodds then asked about the driving position of the man, seated as he was to the left of Evelyn Foster: driving what must have been a distance of twelve miles. What do you say to the possibility of that?'

'I should say it would be a very difficult thing to do. It would be almost an impossibility if she resisted.' Mr Bates, in an attempt to prove that a man was driving the car at this time was to ask: 'A comparatively experienced driver could drive like that?'

'Yes.' Replied Jennings before quickly adding: 'But it would not be by any means safe.' William Jennings then escorted the jury out to inspect a Hudson similar to that of Evelyn's, to demonstrate some of the answers to the questions. The main one being the driving position of the man; in this he received the help of a local hotel keeper, who took up the driving position of Evelyn Foster while the position of the man was acted out by the local Postmaster. With the demonstration over, the evidence of William Jennings came to an end and the hearing also moved into its last phase.

The emphasis now shifted once more to Mr Dodds as he began the summing up of the case. He began with the same warning that he had used earlier against the statement of Evelyn Foster: 'Again, I warn you that the statement is not to be taken as evidence of fact. It has simply been pursued as a line of inquiry to find if there was any fact in the evidence which confirmed it and would bring it home conclusively, not in part, but in entirety. I have no doubt that you have heard many rumours concerned with this case but I ask you to dismiss these rumours from your mind. The doctors are quite agreed that death has been caused by shock due to burns. It is your duty to find out how these burns were sustained.' Mr Dodds went on to point out that it was either a case of murder, accidental death or suicide. On the murder theory he was to note: 'If a man was concerned in this case – without knowing who he was – he appears to me to be a homicidal maniac. Either that or he was doing something to hide something of his own actions.' Mr Dodds then moved on: 'Crimes are committed in very many ways: sometimes for obvious reasons, sometimes for reasons unknown. In this case we are dealing with the question as to whether somebody was implicated, a stranger, or whether the deceased herself did it. Subject to what your opinion is, I think we can eliminate any question of suicide.' Why he decided to eliminate the suicide theory, Mr Dodds, never made clear he only decided it had to be so.

Not only did Mr Dodds rule out the suicide theory, he placed little emphasis on the murder theory either. The majority of his summing up was geared towards the theory that Evelyn Foster had set fire to the car herself: problem was, why did she do it? The main points are, he went on: 'Was the girl murdered or did she set fire to the car and in so doing obtain the burns accidently? If you can answer one of these questions you will have an answer to the case.' One of the main areas to be examined by Mr Dodds was the matter of insurance. The car was covered by two policies, on one of these the car was only covered against anything happening within the garage: this policy, therefore, was to be disregarded. 'You must consider what the girls object would be. Would her object be to obtain the money from the insurance on her car? The other policy does cover a car up to 30 HP and to a value of £700 if it takes fire outside and Mr Foster said in his evidence that this car was covered under that policy. So there would be pecuniary benefit if she wanted to burn her car.'

Mr Dodds went on to address what he described as the 'extraordinary features' of the case as he saw them; mainly these were to centre on such things as the fact that no one had actually seen any 'strange man' in Otterburn, even though some witnesses had passed the car as it came to rest. Evelyn Foster had for some reason, not taken George Philipson on that journey, even though she had said she would, and he had been available at that time. After leaving Otterburn, there had only been one reliable sighting of her car, by John Robson, at Raylees Farm. A witness singled out by Mr Dodds, was John Kennedy who, according to Mr Dodds was; 'A man of remarkable views.' There was also the point that Evelyn Foster, through her mother, had said: 'She had been interfered with' or outraged when the evidence of Professor McDonald proved that she had not. Likewise, Evelyn had stated that both she and her car had been set on fire while the car was still on the road and that she was unconscious at this time. The first she knew was when she heard the 'bump bumping of the car across the moorland. Evidence by both

Insp Russell and William Jennings was to prove otherwise. Mr Dodds then ended his summing up with the words: 'My opinion, I must say, is that I do not think there is sufficient evidence to say that these burns were caused by another person.'

The jury then retired to a small ante room at 4-15 pm there, to deliberate on the evidence of the last few days. It was thought that the deliberation would not take very long, in fact very few left their seats as they thought they would soon be back again. Mr Dodds departed for his tea at the Percy Arms, next door and reporters rushed to telephones to pass on the latest story to their editors. Few thought that the decision would take a long two and a quarter hours to thrash out. The jury finally made it known that they had come to a decision and Mr Dodds was summoned from tea and was ready to take the decision at 6-25 pm. Mr Dodds asked the jury if they had come to a verdict. Mr McDougal, jury foreman, replied in the affirmative and, on being asked, gave the decision: 'The verdict is wilful murder against some person unknown.' The feelings of Mr Dodds at this point are unclear, only the local press informed their readers that he looked surprised. Mr Dodds surprised or not, was then to state: 'I suppose you mean that somebody deliberately poured petrol over her and set her on fire?' Jury foreman, Mr McDougal affirmed that was so. Mr Dodds then proceeded to write down the official statement and then read it to the hearing; 'We, the jury, find that Evelyn Foster died on the 7th day of January, 1931, at the Kennels, Otterburn, from shock due to burns caused by petrol being wilfully thrown over her and ignited by some person or some persons unknown.' With that, the official hearing for the case of Evelyn Foster came to an end. The ramifications however, were about to start.

That there was discord soon became apparent, the following day the press were to launch headlines such as: 'Police and Jury disagree.' Chief Constable Captain Fullarton James had seemingly released a statement to the press giving the views of the police: 'We are satisfied that the motor-car in which Miss Foster's supposed murderer is said to have travelled from Jedburgh, does not exist. We are also satisfied that the man she described does not exist.' Various newspapers were to ask for clarification on the statement however, Fullarton James and the police refused to comply. His refusal was seen, especially by the Fosters, as a confirmation that he had made a statement. One juryman was to state: 'Surely we were in the best position to form an accurate judgement on the case.' Another juryman, George Sinclair, failed to see why his statement, referring to a strange man seen in the village, was not used; as a member of the jury he could not be a witness as well. Feelings in Otterburn were running high in the aftermath of the hearing, mostly aimed at the police.

Joseph Foster was also to air his grievances through the pages of the press, insisting that his daughter had been murdered. He was to refer to the petrol can, saying that he knew his daughter had always carried a 'Pratt's' petrol can; The 'Shell' can, he insisted, had been left by her attacker. He seemingly forgot that he stated at the hearing, that he had not even seen the petrol can for ten days. Joseph Foster was also to attack the coroner's statement in connection with insurance of the car: he was to insist that they would only have received £40 from the insurance claim. John Kennedy was also to jump onto the press bandwagon, stating that the car that had passed him, at so fast a speed it had caused him to noticed it. It had, he went on, no lights on and only put them on when it approached the corner before putting them off again. This, said John Kennedy: 'Shows that he (the man) knew the road.'

George McDougal

With feelings running so high and statements becoming more and more outrageous by the minute, or at least by each issue of newspaper, Joseph Foster, released a further statement to the press that he was going to inform Colonel Douglas Clifton Brown MP, in the hope that he would raise the question, on the Evelyn Foster case, in the House of Commons. The statement in the press began: 'If I ruin my business in pursuing the terrible crime until the murderer is arrested, I shall not hesitate to do it.' The letter, a touch rambling had three questions at its core: 1) Why was my daughters burned car left unprotected for hours so that finger prints could not be taken? 2) It is also a fact that the police made no attempt to check footprints at the scene of the tragedy until the ground had been trampled over by curious spectators. 3) Why was the skill and experience of Scotland Yard ignored by the Northumberland Police? Colonel Douglas Clifton Brown MP, interviewed by the local press, was to state, that, due to being in London he could not attend the hearing. However, he had followed the case with interest. At first he had been convinced it was a straightforward murder now, after weighing up the evidence, he had his doubts.

In Otterburn there was even talk of holding a protest meeting: George McDougal, head gardener at Otterburn Tower and jury foreman was quoted in the press: The jury gave their verdict and it does not matter what the Chief Constable is supposed to have said.' As a result of Joseph Foster's letter to his MP, a committee meeting was held on 24 March, 1931, in the Moot Hall, Newcastle. Captain Fullarton James read his report to the committee: 'With regard to the paragraph in Mr J.J. Foster's letter...alleging that I made a statement on the verdict of the coroner's jury to a newspaper reporter. I wish to say that no such statement was made. I did, however, have what I considered a confidential conversation with a reporter about two hours before the jury returned their verdict. I had no idea that the conversation would be published.' He then carried on but made no reference to the lack of finger printing or footmarks at the crime scene. On the final paragraph of Joseph Foster's letter he was to say: 'It was not considered necessary to obtain the assistance of Scotland Yard.' He went on to further state: 'The police will pursue every line of inquiry likely to lead to a solution of the problems raised by the death of Miss Evelyn Foster.' With the committee meeting over, the police carried on with their work and the case of Evelyn Foster was finally drawn to a close.

Joseph Foster was to state in the local press, sometime after the hearing, that he and some friends had spent a great deal of time trying to trace aspects of the case. They had tried to trace the car that brought the man to Elishaw. They had tried to trace the man: all without success. The Hudson remained in the Foster garage for quite some time, gnawing away at his very soul every day. Joseph Foster was forced to state: 'I have not given up hope entirely, but, I am afraid, the end of a fruitless quest is in sight.'

Notes.

1) The word 'odd' refers to any money over and above the original £200. In £240 odd, the 'Odd' refers to the £40 plus, hence, a few more which would be referred to as 'Odd'.

2) Inspector Edward Russell's statement shows that he arrived at Wolf's Nick at 3-30 pm. Goodman, p 54, states that he arrived shortly before 9 am. He was in
Otterburn at this time.

3) Goodman, p 102, states that Evelyn had two bank accounts: she only had one, with Lloyds Bank, Bellingham. Goodman also states that Evelyn was worth £1,442. This total would appear to also include the car as collateral, a car she no longer had.

4) A 'half crown' piece was a coin slightly larger than a modern-day 10p coin with a value of two-shillings and sixpence.

5) Nipping could be taken as to mean Evelyn was nipped against the side of the car as in squashed, by the weight of the man. The context used by the coroner, and Professor McDonald, was taken to mean, nipped as in pinching between finger and thumb.

CHAPTER SEVEN

CONCLUSIONS: UNRAVELLING THE TANGLED WEB.

We have looked at the story that evolved from the Evelyn Foster case; we have had a glimpse of her background and have studied the arguments and conclusions of the official enquiry into the death of Evelyn Foster. The whole thing put together, however, leaves more questions than answers. The main query begins with the evidence given by Evelyn Foster herself. Her statement provides the backbone for the whole of what occurred on the night of 6 January, 1931. The main drawback is that her evidence is almost wholly unsupported by any other witness. We have to take her evidence wholly on the trust of Evelyn Foster or leave it. The latter, is the rather odd conclusion that the coroner took: at the official enquiry, he decreed that the statement of Evelyn Foster was inadmissible as evidence of fact. Anyone studying the case is now left with the belief that the statement of Evelyn Foster was nothing more than pure fabrication from the start. If this was in a court of law, and Evelyn Foster was on trial, then she would be deemed as guilty from the outset before the trial had even started.

The whole statement by Evelyn Foster revolves around the *man* she says she picked up at Elishaw Road Ends after he had flagged her down. The car he had arrived in sat at the road ends directly in the beam of the headlights of Evelyn's Hudson: a car she was later to describe as a hard top saloon. She noted that two other occupants were in the car, one of which was a woman sitting in the driving seat. Evelyn Foster knew almost every inch of the Otterburn district; she had lived there for twenty-nine years and had driven around it for some fourteen years. She also knew most people in the district and even knew their cars. Cars were her business as well as her interest and most of their owners in the district made use of her father's garage. In her statement, she recognised the car of Mr Kirsopp Reed, as it travelled north from Belsay in the dark. If the car or its driver at Elishaw Road Ends had been local then Evelyn would surely have recognised them as such. The fact that Evelyn did not recognise the woman is almost proof positive that she was not local or that she too was a figment of Evelyn's imagination. [1]

At least she left a description of the car. Two witnesses, Albert Beach and Robert Townes, also saw a car that had seemingly stopped at Elishaw Road Ends. The only problem was their description did not fit with that given by Evelyn. In fact, although these men were only a hundred or so yards apart, their descriptions were for two different cars: Albert Beach stated it was a two-seater, whilst Robert Townes noted it was a soft-top touring car.[2] The statement by Albert Beach was used at the enquiry while the statement by Robert Townes was not. The problem is, Evelyn's car was not the only one in the vicinity of Elishaw Road Ends at that time.

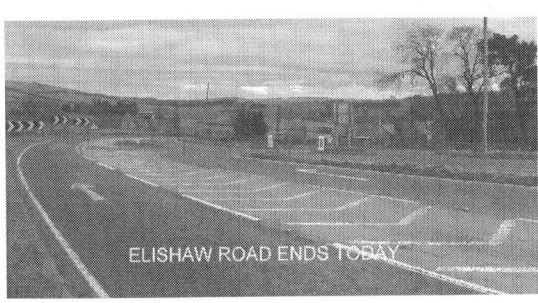
ELISHAW ROAD ENDS TODAY

Landlord of the 'Redesdale Arms', Ben Prior, reported to the police that three well dressed strangers entered the hotel at around 6-30 pm and left around 7 pm. These men, he was to note, were in an Essex car, a car not that dissimilar from Evelyn's Hudson and made by the same company. Although Ben Prior took little notice, he did note that the registration number had a '2' in it and the letters were TN, the same as Evelyn's, the registration letters of Newcastle upon Tyne. Ben Prior was also to note that, the three men had Scottish accents. Leaving the Redesdale Arms at around 7 pm, this car must have passed Elishaw Road Ends at around 7-05 pm, whether it travelled via Otterburn of Dere Street is not known however, it must have raised the hopes of the police more than a little - they were to be short lived. After hearing the request, on the radio, the owner of the car, who came from Doncaster, reported to the local police. His passengers, both from Chester Le Street, did likewise and the car and its passengers were eliminated from the police enquiries. The question remains, could this car have been the one seen by both Albert Beach and Robert Townes?

MAUGHANS VIEW FROM THE CO-OP TO THE KENNELS

One of the main reasons advanced by many, that the *man* was never found was that he may have told Evelyn lies. To even consider this we have first to accept Evelyn's statement as a true account and only the *man* lied to her. It is possible of course however; we have to believe Evelyn implicitly to the detriment of all others. The plain fact was, no one else saw a *strange man* in the vicinity of Evelyn's Hudson or, for that matter, the Kennels. George Maughan was the closest to Evelyn's Hudson and he saw no one but a woman sitting in the driver's seat. Robert Luke was the second closest person to Evelyn's Hudson; he saw nothing either of any person even though he lingered longer than George Maughan, as he searched for some wire to carry out a job. Of the other witnesses, John Thompson, claimed that he saw George Maughan as well as Evelyn standing at the petrol pump outside the Kennels. In actual fact, because of timings, he saw neither.[3]

George Sinclair, respected manager of the local Co-Op, also saw a man skulking near the Post Office. He could tell it was a man and could tell he was a stranger to Otterburn yet, he could not see the man's face. Of the two teachers, Mary Ferry and Annie Carruthers, they just saw a man, it could have been any man and either of these men could have been George Philipson who was known to have been on the street at that time and, like the *man* he appears to have been unseen by anyone. When Mary Ferry saw the *man* Evelyn's Hudson was well on the way to Raylees Farm. Annie Carruthers said the man she saw became offensive and made suggestive remarks yet; she never really said what the man had said to her or how the man appeared offensive to her. The members of staff of the Percy Arms, where the *man* was supposed to go, saw nothing of him and, neither did they see any sign of Evelyn who was supposed to meet the *man* there.

Most of what has been published so far, about the Evelyn Foster case, has blamed one source for not reaching any conclusion; the police. This, however, is a totally unfair assessment and, it has to be said, was generated by the press intent on finding a story at whatever the cost. The Northumberland County Constabulary were a bit behind the times, that cannot be denied, however, there is one point that is much missed. The police turned up with the knowledge that they were looking at a murder case, a suspect, they were sure, would be found in a reasonably short time. Within a couple of days it became painfully obvious to the police that they were wrong. The fact that not only were the suspects not found, there was no sign of any at all, not even the slightest lead had been found in the hunt for the missing car. From this moment on, the police knew this was no longer a murder enquiry, the doubts were there and the enquiries were now geared to the problem of why and how Evelyn Foster had fired the car herself.

No one, police, press or other had advanced a theory as to what time the fire had actually been started. The answer to that question lay with a shepherd, Sidney Henderson, who lived in a shepherds dwelling at Harwood Head. Sidney Henderson had set off to walk from Harwood Head to Harwood Gate, a distance of some three miles, along the Elsdon to Morpeth road. About midway along the road Sidney Henderson, looked across the moor to his right and saw a fire in the vicinity of Wolf's Nick. The time, he noted, was 8-45 pm and the fire was burning brightly giving the appearance that the fire had just started. From this road there is an uninterrupted view of Wolf's Nick. In the dark, the fire would have caught his eye within a short time of starting. It is reasonable to assume that the fire started at around 8-45 pm give or take a few minutes either way. Sidney Henderson assumed that the fire was caused by a car which may have crashed off the road. Wolf's Nick is two miles from the point where Sidney Henderson was standing when he first viewed the fire. When he arrived at Harwood Gate, it was 9 pm, he looked across and noted that the fire had by then died down. Sidney Henderson was not questioned about it and no emphasis was placed on his evidence. This is an odd omission as the statement, if the times were noted, proved beyond all doubt that Evelyn Foster never travelled as far as Belsay; she simply did not have the time. In itself, this was a damning statement against Evelyn Foster proving that she did not travel much further than Wolf's Nick. [4]

RAYLEES FARM TOWARDS OTTERBURN TODAY

The police maintained the theory that Evelyn Foster did not drive as far as Belsay, in fact, went no further than Wolf's Nick. The only reliable sighting and timing of her car had been at Raylees Farm at 7-22 pm. Evelyn left Otterburn at around 7-15 pm, the timing gives her speed of around sixteen miles per hour in covering the two miles. This appears to be about normal given the speeds of other road users that night. Travelling at this speed she would have reached Wolf's Nick at around 7-37 pm, making allowances for her speed of ten miles per hour at Raylees Farm and the climbing, twisting terrain to Wolf's nick. Given the average speed of the Hudson as around sixteen miles per hour, over the eleven miles to Belsay and back to Wolf's Nick, a total of some twenty-two miles, the trip would have taken around one hour and twenty-two minutes. Even moving her average speed up another couple of miles per hour Evelyn could not have driven to Belsay and back to Wolf's Nick in that period of time. The police also arrived at this conclusion and demolished the idea that she drove as far as Belsay at all. For some reason they failed to offer any proof of this, even though they were in passion of it. Along with the other doubts that had appeared in her statement, the police concluded there had been no murder.

If Evelyn Foster had not driven as far as Belsay then the question that becomes obvious is, where did she go? Given her average speed of fourteen miles per hour, and there is no reason for believing she drove any faster, she could only have driven as far as Ferney Chesters road end, some five miles short of Belsay, and back again. This would allow her to get back to Wolf's nick and fit in with, the timing of a burning car at Wolf's Nick, given by Sidney Henderson: his evidence cannot be denied, only one car was found burned at Wolf's Nick. Kirsopp Reed was on the road at around this time and, he was to state, that he passed Tate's bus at Ferney Chesters. Evelyn's Hudson was, as we have seen, some way behind Tait's bus and, Kirsopp Reed was further to state, he passed no other vehicle after he passed the bus.

Evelyn Foster topped up the petrol tank on her car before she left Otterburn. Just how much petrol she put in is impossible to know: the book in which she recorded such transactions was burned with the car. The petrol tank on the Hudson held fifteen gallons. When William Jennings inspected the car, the ends of the rear springs, on which the petrol tank rested, were bent down some four inches due to the weight of the petrol tank in the heat of the fire. This indicated to Jennings that a considerable amount of petrol had been in the tank at the time of the fire. The fullness of the petrol tank would also indicate that Evelyn had not driven very far. We can only assume that, if Evelyn did not drive to Belsay then she parked the Hudson somewhere along the road where it could not be seen.

If we are to accept Evelyn Foster's statement then we acknowledge that she was attacked by the man in the vicinity of Belsay. The man then drove the car northwards, sitting in what can only be described as an impossible position for driving. The relative impossibility of driving a car in this fashion was shown by William Jennings. The man then drove the Hudson eleven miles in this position to a place he had no knowledge of whatever, Wolf's Nick. The fact that he stopped there begs the question why that spot? He then viciously attacked Evelyn once more before throwing something over her and setting fire to both her and the car. No one has said what this substance was or what it was carried in. A man dressed in the manner that Evelyn described would hardly be carrying a can of petrol in his pocket. If this was so, where did he hide it when he got in the taxi? There certainly would have been a smell. One person who believed in this theory was Joseph Foster: this theory can best be described as barmy. Professor McDonald has shown that Evelyn bore none of the marks that would be expected if she had suffered such an attack from any man.

Again, in believing Evelyn's version, she had been attacked on a second occasion reducing her to a semi conscious state before something was thrown over her and then ignited. The first Evelyn knew was when she felt the car, 'bump, bumping' over the moor. She had been sitting in the back of the car, however, if she had been in the rear of the car, as well as in a semi conscious state, she would surely have been thrown forward, when the car nose-dived over the four foot embankment, and probably onto the floor or at least, along the rear seat. Lying in any one of these positions would have resulted in different burns to those that she suffered. Professor McDonald merely stated that she had been in a sitting position on a straight edge, this could have been either seat or running board. Professor McDonald, William Jennings and Inspector Russell all reached the conclusion that the car was not on fire when it dropped down the embankment but, was set on fire where it stood, on the moor.

If we do not accept the statement of Evelyn Foster then, she had parked her Hudson somewhere within the area of Wolf's Nick. She then drove it or allowed it to run onto the moor before setting fire to it. It is not however, so simple. If the car had been driven onto the moor simply to get rid of it or to make it look like an accident; then it would have been driven off the road at a slightly less angle without worrying what happened to it after it left the road. The car, however, was deliberately manoeuvred so that it would hit the top of the embankment at right angles to the road; this manoeuvre points to another reason of why the car was set on fire: a deliberate act rather than accident. The tyre marks on the frosted road, pointing to this manoeuvring, were as plain as any finger print.

The heavy frost on the road had left the tyre marks on the road surface pointing the finger towards the demise of the car. This would not be so obvious to the perpetrator in the dark. Both Inspector Russell and William Jennings had made notes of these. Sometime after it came to a halt at Wolf's Nick, the car was deliberately turned so that it was at right angles to the road edge. There is only one reason for this manoeuvre and that was to eliminate the chance of the car rolling onto its side as it went over the edge of the embankment. This would suggest the actions of someone who wanted to draw attention to the car on the moor yet, did not want it out of sight of the road, as it would have been if it had rolled over.

Once the fire had died down, probably within twenty to thirty minutes, the car would have been out of sight; let it roll across the moor and it would have been visible for far longer, increasing the chances of it being observed by some passerby. It is highly doubtful if anyone had been at the wheel at the time the car went over the embankment. William Jennings was to note: 'If someone was at the wheel of the car then they had lost interest in driving it.' Evelyn knew what time the bus would pass Wolf's Nick: did she deliberately place the car in the best position for it to be seen on the moor by Cecil Johnstone?

THE BURNT HUDSON

There were three reasons to be considered as to the cause of Evelyn Foster's death: murder, suicide or accident. Suicide was immediately ruled out by coroner Mr Dodd's, although he gave no reason for doing so. The murder theory was put to the test during the hearing and was found wanting to say the least. The main argument against the murder theory was the fact that there was no evidence of a third party, man or woman, to be found. The evidence advanced by Professor McDonald proved, beyond all doubt that, Evelyn carried no injuries from any physical attack by any other person. Although Evelyn had stated, via her mother, that she had been 'interfered with' therefore suggesting sexual molestation, there was no evidence of that either. Mr Dodds had disallowed Evelyn Foster's statement as 'evidence of fact'; in his eyes it became unbelievable. The evidence moved further and further away from the murder theory as the main witnesses gave their statements. This was further reinforced by Mr Dodds in his summing up when he stated: 'My opinion, I must say, is that I do not think there is sufficient evidence to say that her burns were caused by another person.' The evidence now appeared to point towards the theory that the fire and resulting burns were self inflicted. If she had caused the fire herself, deliberately or accidental, what was the motif?

It had been suggested that Evelyn had set fire to the car in order to gain money from the insurance. It had further been suggested that Evelyn could claim quite an amount, up to £700 maximum. She did have an amount in the Bank and a savings account, a total of around £490. Question is, what did she need the money for and was it enough to risk death for? Quite rightly, no one, apart from Evelyn, had the answer to that. What is missing is any evidence at all of any incomings and outgoings as well as expenses concerning her taxi business. All of this, rather unbelievably, was kept in a single notebook, with no duplicate at all, and that notebook went up in flames with the car. Questioned about this by Mr Dodds, Evelyn's father could cast no light on her expenses at all only noting that, he 'believed' that she, Evelyn, only had that one account book and; 'As a rule it was kept in the car.'. [5] According to the evidence of Joseph Foster, Evelyn helped keep the books for the garage business presumably in a better state of order than her own.

Although the murder and accident theories were much discussed, not only during the hearing but also in the press, one other area was only hinted at by Mr Dodds and, just as quickly as it appeared, it was brushed under the carpet. Mr Dodds was to note in his summing up: 'There are cases where a person becomes obsessed, for some inexplicable reason, with the idea either of gaining notoriety or of doing something abnormal.' The police, at least in the form of Capt

Fullarton James, were to share this opinion. Fullarton James was to state: 'I believe the girl set fire to the car herself...I think it more than likely, as the coroner suggested, that she was a hysterical girl who was obsessed with a desire for publicity or that she was suffering from some abnormality.' Therefore, two people at least thought that Evelyn had fired the car herself for the purpose of notoriety or she was abnormal in that she suffered some mental derangement.

Obviously, the Doctors who had attended Evelyn would have known if there were any mental problems in Evelyn's background, neither commented on that but, neither seemed to be asked either. We certainly cannot tell at this distance in time. It should, in all fairness, be stated that no one knows exactly what goes on in another person's mind as far as mental problems are concerned. However, as we are looking at the case through a historical perspective we can look at events outside the official reports or, at least use these reports as guidance.

There are, perhaps, two main parts of the Evelyn Foster case that stick out in an almost extraordinary fashion yet, oddly, they are normally shied away from. Firstly there is what happened to the car in the last few minutes of its journey. Was it set on fire on the road or on the moor? Evidence points strongly to the latter. Both of these questions are interesting points and can be open to interpretation depending on who you read. The evidence, given at the hearing is quite clear and is set out earlier. One of the main queries, however, is the positioning of the car on the road, as already discussed. The car was deliberately turned across the road, almost to the point of fussiness and the only reason for this is the fact that, approaching the embankment head on it would not roll over after it's decent. A mere yard or so further on and the story would have been completely different as the terrain further along the embankment drops so quickly.

This is certainly not a murderer's way of getting rid of a car, that would have been straight on and over the embankment further on; certainly, on a first look the car would have then had the appearance of crashing off the road, no suspicious circumstances. With the car rolled over and on fire, he or she would want to make good their escape as soon as possible and get away from the scene. The second thing of note is probably more subjective; however, it may have more bearing on the Foster case than almost anything else: this is the locality.

In this area of Northumberland there were, and are, literally thousands of places in which getting rid of a car, without being disturbed in the act, would be a very simple matter indeed. It has been noted by one author, Julian Symons, writing on the Foster case, that getting rid of a car was not so simple. Writing about Wolf's Nick as a chosen spot he was to state: 'At that time, however, there was practically no other spot along this road where a car could have been driven on to the moor.' This is, of course, highly inaccurate and misleading. Taking the road from Belsay, north towards Otterburn, open fields, which would offer such a hiding place, literally litter the roadsides offering a quiet place to get rid of a car surreptitiously. From Knowesgate to Otterburn, some eleven miles, the road to either side is wide open moor and any part of it could be quite easily accessed for the disposal of a car. The same author has, however, offered us one of the most telling of statements when he wrote of the *Invisible man*: 'He obviously had very considerable local knowledge'. More than once this statement was to be heard during the period of the hearing, especially by witnesses but, also in the local press. Joseph Foster and witness John Kennedy to name but two gave in their statements, that the person involved had 'considerable local knowledge'.

The area where Evelyn Foster's car was found lies just over one hundred yards to the north of a point known locally as Wolf's Nick. The word *locally* is important as Wolf's Nick does not even appear on any maps. The nearest thing is Wolf Crag, a local climbing spot, about one mile to the north of Wolf's Nick. To drive along the Otterburn to Newcastle road, in either direction, you would drive passed Wolf's Nick without giving it a second glance. This is the point that Evelyn Foster's statement would have us believe, the *man*, a stranger to the area, picked out on a dark winter's night, to carry out a murder. There are people, even today and who live within a couple of miles of the area, if asked directions for Wolf's Nick would give you a blank look. To pick out Wolf's Nick, for whatever reason, a person would have to be in possession of what some statement's referred to as considerable local knowledge. There is one thing we can say with certainty; Evelyn Foster had considerable local knowledge.

She had been brought up in the area of Otterburn and, since the age of fifteen, had driven around that area. Much of her time was also spent as a conductress on the Foster busses and the majority of her journeys took her along the Otterburn to Newcastle route that led past Wolf's Nick. Her life as a taxi driver also helped to broaden her horizons on the local area front and she must have driven past Wolf's Nick many countless times. She was also known to have taken local children from Otterburn on outings into the countryside; it would be interesting to know if any of these outings included journey's to Wolf's Nick.

Even today, Wolf's Nick, must look just as it did in 1931. In daylight it does stick out against the moorland landscape as it dominates the skyline, approached from both directions, as it stands on the highest point of the road. A closer look brings one aspect to mind, it looks like a stage set. Approaching from the north, the rocky outcrop forms a backdrop; the road and its embankment forms a cut off point to the west while the front opens out with a view, northwards, that takes in the Ottercops hills and Winter's gibbet, some two miles off, above Elsdon while beyond is open moorland stretching to the distant Cheviot Hills. Put together, the feeling is immediately of an amphitheatre. Could this have been seen by Evelyn Foster as an Amphitheatre of death, a final stage on which to act out the demise of her car and possibly herself? It certainly bears thinking about given the evidence of her hearing as well as the comments by the coroner, Mr Dodds and Fullarton James, on 'crimes of notoriety'.

THE KENNELS TODAY

With the end of Evelyn Foster's story, we can now take a look at how it has been presented over the intervening years. A main source, for any reader, has to be the book by Jonathan Goodman; 'The Burning Of Evelyn Foster' published in 1977. Goodman covered the story well and his book only suffered in the fact that he had no access to the official documentation of the hearing; these being locked away in the Northumberland Archives under the seventy-five rule. His book also lacking in the more minor point that, he did not have what Evelyn Foster had, local knowledge. Only travelling to Northumberland two or three times is a huge handicap when trying to piece a complex story together. Julian Symons also dedicated one chapter of his book; 'A Reasonable Doubt' published 1960, to the Foster case. The chapter, under the heading: 'The Invisible Man' naturally concentrates on the hunt for the *man*, and, therefore, sets out to treat the Foster case as a murder with no consideration at all for any other result. Most of the press, local, national and international covered the story well during the period apart, that is, from the odd one or two that came up with some odd conclusions that really beggared belief.

Over the intervening years, the story of Evelyn Foster has made the odd appearance mostly in the press, occasionally on local television. Local coverage, however, usually covers the case from the murder angle only with the main thrust of their argument being, the *strange man*. No reason or thought being aired on any other angle that may have happened. Over the years this attitude has only served to add to the continuing legend and myth of the Evelyn Foster case. Television drama has, so far, given us only one representation of the Evelyn Foster case. This appeared in the: '*In Suspicious Circumstances*', series under the title of: '*The Man Who*

FOSTER GARAGE TODAY

Melted Away', an ITV production of January 1994. Once more, as the title suggests, the programme centres on the aspect of the *man*. The drama bears little relation to what happened on the Twelfth Night of 1931 at all and only the characters names are recognisable. The whole programme is what has become known as 'faction' in that it is fiction woven around a true event and makes dismal viewing as far as the real story goes.

There is one further twist in the tail of the Evelyn Foster Case; this was introduced by Jonathan Goodman. A man named Ernest Brown, was tried, convicted and executed, in Armley Gaol, Leeds in February, 1934 for the murder of Frederick Ellison Morton the previous year. Brown shot his boss, Morton, then attempted to destroy the body by placing it in Morton's car and setting fire to it. On the scaffold, Ernest Brown is thought to have said, when asked by the prison chaplain if he had anything to say, either, 'Ought to burn' or 'Otterburn'. However, emphasis should be placed on the word *thought* as there is no proof of what he said at all. Although it looks convincing with its similarity to the car fire, Ernest Brown shot Fred Morton first: he only used the car fire to get rid of the body. If he had murdered Evelyn Foster, he would have made sure she was dead and that the body was suitably disposed of, both the car and occupant well and truly burned away to the point of total destruction.

On the Otterburn theory, supposedly uttered by Ernest brown, there is also an Otterburn in the North Riding of Yorkshire, near Settle. The Yorkshire Otterburn is a mere twenty or so miles from Tadcaster where Ernest Brown murdered Fred Morton. However, as with all legends and myths, it has caught on with the public, mainly through the modern-day internet and Ernest Brown has become, without any foundation at all, the recognised murderer of Evelyn Foster. At best, the Ernest Brown theory should only be viewed as making a piece in order to fit a jigsaw puzzle so that they can provide a convenient ending that fits the murder theory. In reality it has little if any foundation or substance to connect it with the death of Evelyn Foster. [6]

In modern-day Otterburn, eighty years after the event, the people are divided as to what happened on the Twelfth Night of 1931. Some are reluctant to mention it while for others the normal answer appears to be: 'No one really knows, nothing was proved.' The

'Kennels' today stands almost derelict almost a memorial to one of its more known residents. A few yards down the street, there is no difficulty in finding the grave of Evelyn Foster; it stands just inside the gate with the family name Foster on its back while emblazoned on its front is the name of Evelyn Foster, complete with incorrect age, and her sister, Margaret Elizabeth. The original kerb stones have gone from the graves to facilitate the grass cutting and general maintenance of the churchyard. Sharing the churchyard are a few other names that also appear in the strange case of Evelyn Foster.

Jonathan Goodman closed his book with the observation that, a holly wreath was placed on Evelyn Foster's grave every Christmas and removed on the Twelfth Night, the anniversary of her death. This practice has now stopped, probably due to the fact that the last of the Foster family has left Otterburn. Certainly, no wreath has been placed on her grave in the last eight years and the present incumbent has no knowledge of this ceremony ever taking place. History, piece by piece, is gradually closing its wings over one of the more known former residents of Otterburn.

Notes.

1) It is important to note that Evelyn Foster recognised the driver of the car at Elishaw as a woman, however, she did not recognise the woman. If this driver had been Mrs Charlotte Clark, Evelyn would surely have recognised her as Charlotte Clark had lived at Troughend Hall for over eleven years at that time.

2) Statements by Albert Beach and Robert Townes. Northumberland Archives COS/3/54/1. It seems difficult to say why the statement of Albert Beach was used in the hearing and that of Robert Townes was not.

3) Statement by John Thompson. Northumberland Archives COS/3/54/1. His statement clearly states that he left work at 7 pm and entered Otterburn at 7 15 pm. George Maughan had left Otterburn at 7 pm. Clearly John Thompson could not have met George Maughan at that time. A piece was added to his statement at a later date in which he said: 'I am sure the man I met was Maughan, at the time'.

4) The statement of Sidney Henderson was heard at the hearing; the odd thing was It was not queried and no attachment of importance was given to it yet, this was the only clear proof of when the fire actually started. It certainly would have proved at the time that Evelyn Foster did not and could not drive to Belsay in the times given.

5) That there were no duplicate accounts appears to be very odd. The remains of Evelyn Foster's notebook was recovered from under the driver's seat of her taxi. No evidence was ever put forward if anything at all could be read from the remains of the notebook.

6) The Ernest Brown murder was very different from that of Evelyn Foster. It was a disposal of a body after the murder had been committed as opposed to a murder by fire.

SELECT BIBLIOGRAPHY.

Cruster. H. H.   'A History Of Northumberland Vol 8' Andrew Reid & Co 1907.

"   "   "   "   Vol 9   "
"   1908.

Dodds. J.F.   'Bastions and Belligerents: Medieval Strongholds In Northumberland.
                   Keepdate Publishing Ltd 1999.

Fraser. G.M. 'The Steel Bonnets'   Pan Books   1974.

Goodman. Jonathan.   'The Burning Of Evelyn Foster'.   David & Charles.   1977.

Hodgson J.   'A History Of Northumberland Vol 2'   Frank Graham facsimile. 1973.

McCutcheon. J.E.　　'The Hartley Colliery Disaster'.
McCutcheon.　　1963.

Ridley. N.　　'Northumbrian Heritage'　　Robert Hale. 1968.

"　　"　　'Portrait Of Northumberland'.　　"　　" 1969.

Symons Julian.　　'A Reasonable Doubt'.　　The Cresset Press.　　1960.

Tomlinson. W. W.　　'A Guide To Northumberland'.　　David & Charles.　　1968.

Murder Casebook Series.　　'Trial by Coroner: Philip Drew and Evelyn Foster'.

Marshall Cavendish.　　1991.

PHOTOGRAPH CREDITS.

Foster Family: P 17, 19, 21, 23, 27, 32.

Local Press: P 43, 56, 80, 101, 102, 104, 108, 116, 121, 131.

Trish ? In Canada: P 58.

Author: P 59, 111, 125, 126, 128, 135, 136, 139.

Printed in Great Britain
by Amazon.co.uk, Ltd.,
Marston Gate.